The JEWELER'S
STUDIO HANDBOOK

QUARRY

The
JEWELER'S
STUDIO HANDBOOK

Traditional and
Contemporary Techniques
for Working with Metal
and Mixed-Media Materials

BEVERLY MASSACHUSETTS

QUARRY BOOKS

Brandon Holschuh

First published in the United States of America by
Quarry Books, a member of
Quayside Publishing Group
100 Cummings Center
Suite 406-L
Beverly, Massachusetts 01915-6101
Telephone: (978) 282-9590
Fax: (978) 283-2742
www.quarrybooks.com

Library of Congress Cataloging-in-Publication Data
Holschuh, Brandon.
  Jeweler's studio handbook : traditional and contemporary techniques for working with metal and mixed media materials / Brandon Holschuh.
      p. cm.
  Includes index.
  ISBN-13: 978-1-59253-485-2
  ISBN-10: 1-59253-485-6
1. Jewelry making--Handbooks, manuals, etc. I. Title.
  TS740.H65 2009
  739.27--dc22

                                                    2008031600
                                                    CIP

ISBN-13: 978-1-59253-485-2
ISBN-10: 1-59253-485-6
10 9 8 7 6 5 4

Design: Laura H. Couallier, Laura Herrmann Design
Photography: Dan Morgan/www.aboutdanmorgan.com
unless otherwise indicated
Illustrations: Robert Leanna II

Printed in Singapore

For Michelle and Meena

Contents

Riveted Bead Ring,
page 104

Open-Band Copper
Bracelet, page 128

Creation is existent within a critical region of material, thought, and process. All is passing. Meaning cannot be suspended and tension is always present. Jewelry objects have a powerful residue of emotion. Still, everything becomes thin and the ideal object remains thought undefined.

Artist: Todd Pownell
Title: *Hidden Halo*
Materials: Diamonds, gold, sterling, aquamarine, sapphire
Techniques: Fabricated, constructed, soldered, fused

Foreword *by Todd Pownell*

The construction of jewelry involves a compressed attitude toward objects and their use: putting together raw, drifting, and partially formed material from an understanding of their innate qualities through a compiling and composition of these partial materials. The jewelry maker conspires with scattered pieces to produce an object that invites wanderings by being worn on the body.

The Jewelry Object

The jewelry object must produce wonder by engaging and enticing the eye in play and hypnotism into exploration and journeys. The joy of motion trumping the melancholy of unrelenting change is the drama of jewelry. Jewelry is for the finding of desires into nomadic thought as well as tangible voyages through visual forms. The desire to pin or wear jewelry objects on a vacant body is to generate a mini-environment or a portal into unexplored territories via the wearer. Jewelry should never be a mere subject for decoration. Jewelry is exploration and intimacy together.

The Jewelry Maker

The jewelry making process is also an intimate exploration. It begins with the gathering of things and proceeds with organization, cutting, drilling, and linking together. A quality jewelry maker succeeds with relentless attention and an honest strive to proceed and produce.

Brandon Holschuh is such a maker. His work is imbued with both exploration and intimacy and succeeds in transporting both the wearer and viewer into new and different worlds of perception.

An intimate look into a jewelry studio such as his is a rarity and a shared luxury, which is sure to give new insights to jewelry makers of all levels.

TODD POWNELL began his jewelry studies at the Bowman Technical School in Lancaster, Pennsylvania, where he gained an in-depth exposure to jewelry making. During his training he also completed the GIA graduate course in Gemology. He excelled in the craft of jewelry making and went on to a successful career in fine jewelry. Todd's love for the material led him to make his own explorations which have evolved into a large body of work that reflects his own inquiries as an artist.

Introduction

Jewelry artists have the unique ability to bend perception, push limits, and redefine wearable art. Personal adornment is a broad, diverse, and limitless craft. Original, inventive, and artistically designed—this is what makes great jewelry.

We all create objects that speak volumes about our innermost feelings and thoughts. To create work that speaks louder than words, though, you need a foundation, which is why this book is in your hands. *The Jeweler's Studio Handbook* teaches you the core techniques, introduces you to the materials, and hands you the tools needed to flourish in the jewelry-making studio.

In these pages you will tour the artisan studio, inside and out, learning along the way how to express yourself through the tactile, versatile, and ancient craft of making metal jewelry. Illustrating everything from drill bits to silvermith's hammers and onward to scores of nontraditional materials, the pages of this book are rich, hardworking, and inspiring.

For me, writing gives me the same feeling of creation that making jewelry does, sharing my experiences and teaching the processes and techniques. This book is an opportunity for me to communicate to you the same ideas my work conveys visually … and I learn more and more about the craft *myself* along the way. The rush of ideas that stems from teaching, the questions you might not always think to ask of yourself—both enrich you as artist and as teacher.

I encourage you to experiment. Learn from your mistakes. There is inherent value in creating the unexpected; you will always learn best by trying and doing. May *The Jeweler's Studio Handbook* refine your skills, better your designs, and facilitate your creative process.

Outfitting the
Jeweler's
Studio

A spacious, organized, and well-lit studio
ensures enjoyable work. Be sure to think
through your placement of the jeweler's
bench; you will inevitably spend the most
time there. Placement near a window
works well for ventilation and a view.

Planning the Layout
of the Studio

Before choosing the location of your studio, you may want to spend some time reviewing your needs. Space considerations are important, but availability of resources and important health and safety factors should enter into your decision as well. While some jewelers may choose to set up their workbench in a compact corner of the living area, others may prefer to set up in an entire room, or even to rent a work space outside the home. When considering any of these decisions, ask yourself the following questions:

How much time will I spend in this space?
The time spent in your jewelry-making work space will determine where in your house it is located, or whether it's located in your house at all.

Does this space have ample access to resources?
As you begin to outfit your studio, you will notice a greater need for electrical outlets, access to running water, and ample, varied lighting.

Will I be able to grow in this space?
You may quickly find yourself wanting or needing to purchase additional or more advanced equipment. It is best to prepare for this early on.

Space Considerations

As the fundamentals of the jeweler's studio become more familiar, it will become apparent that an overall sense of order is beneficial. The space should accommodate a natural flow of work during and between projects. Having a good organizational system in the studio will minimize stress, facilitate creative thinking, and save considerable time and energy in the long run.

It is always a good idea to outfit the studio with a designated worktable and a workbench. Jeweler's workbenches typically measure about 4 feet (1.2 m) wide and 2 feet (60 cm) deep. Standard work tables usually measure 6 feet (1.8 m) wide and 4 feet (1.2 m) deep. A basic studio layout, shown below, includes space considerations for advanced techniques that require additional equipment and workbenches. Also, consider additional areas of the studio to be designated task zones. Zones may include a desk for paperwork, a computer, a filing cabinet, a packaging area (if you plan to sell your work), and a setup for photography.

Choosing a Location

ELECTRICITY

Lighting and a number of the tools and equipment used in making jewelry require electricity. It is important not to overload your available resources. Be sure to choose a location with enough available lighting or wall outlets for additional lighting. As you begin to use

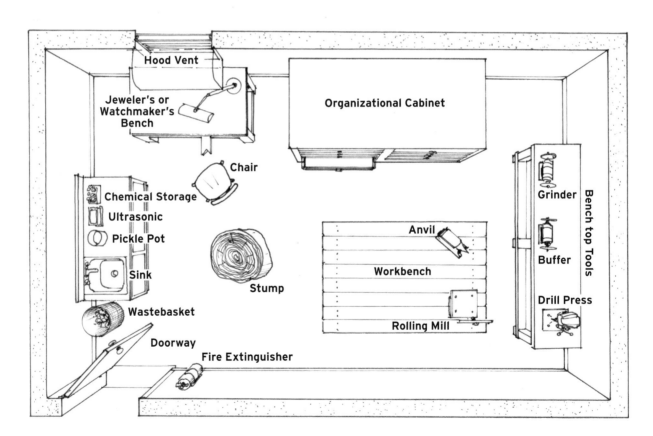

This sample studio layout shows typical work areas such as a tree stump for resistance hammering, a wet area with a sink, and a heavy worktable with benchtop tools.

Workbenches should be sturdy with equipment mounted directly to the work surface with large carriage bolts or lag screws. Pictured from left to right: wet and dry grinders, buffer fitted with tapered spindles, buffing machine with hood and filter, and bench-top drill press.

advanced tools and equipment for a broader range of techniques, avoid overloading your wall power outlets. Most home electrical fires begin with overloaded circuits or faulty wiring of expanded circuits. Consult an electrician to assist you with your needs.

TEMPERATURE

Ideally, you want to be in a controlled indoor climate with a comfortable ambient temperature at all times. Blowing fans in a hot studio will hinder your ability to perform some techniques. The same goes for stand-alone fuel or ceramic heaters in a cold studio; they may not suffice when working with various materials.

WATER

Running water is a necessity in a well-outfitted studio. A standard jeweler's studio is equipped with an arsenal of chemicals, most of which can be neutralized quickly with water. After certain processes, you will need to rinse off your work. Additionally, your metals may sometimes need to be quenched in cool water or debris, dirt, and oils may need to be washed from yourself and your projects. If you must use a sink in another area of your home, such as your kitchen, use caution when rinsing and disposing of chemicals to avoid contaminating your dishes and utensils.

A concentrated light source at the workbench is crucial (above). A mix of types of lighting (fluorescent, halogen [left], incandescent, etc.) may be beneficial. Work will look different under different lights, especially when surface treatments and finishes are applied.

Planning the Work Area

A WELL-LIGHTED PLACE

A great studio is a well-lit studio. Ask any interior designer what the most important element in a work space is and they will surely tell you it is lighting. A combination of desktop and floor lamps may suffice if the work area is small. If the work space is a full-size room or a basement, additional lighting may need to be professionally installed. Large flood lights are ideal for overall lighting, but track lighting will add focused, direct light at task zones. A concentrated, powerful light source is recommended for the jeweler's main workbench.

Advancements in energy-efficient lighting offer adequate illumination while reducing your energy costs. Standard (incandescent) bulbs produce dull, yellow light, however, the bright white or blue/white light emitted by halogen and fluorescent bulbs ease eye strain, which is especially helpful in jewelry making. A combination of multiple lamps may be a good solution for illuminating the work area. (Be careful not to overload your circuits, and never use bulbs that are rated beyond a fixture's capacity.)

FLOORING

You will find when working with metals, there are undoubtedly times that you will drop tools, spill chemicals, and generally abuse your studio floors. Concrete is the safest, most durable flooring option. Alternative materials are hardwood, laminate, ceramic, vinyl and linoleum. Carpeting is not recommended because it can be flammable and will get very dirty, very fast.

AIR QUALITY

When choosing your location, consider the air quality and its relation to the rest of your home. Soldering fumes can easily travel through floor boards above your work area. Simple exhaust systems are relatively easy to install if your studio is located against an outside wall (see page 20). You do not want to perform any soldering or use chemicals in your kitchen.

Hazardous fumes and dangerous smoke can sometimes occur during soldering, especially if using paste-style solders. Be sure to have proper ventilation or wear a respirator.

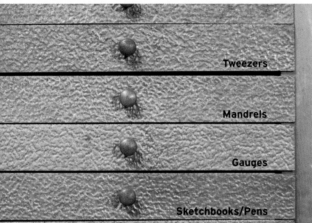

ORGANIZING TOOLS AND MATERIALS

With all the small parts, fine tools, and other eclectic materials required in jewelry making, clutter can accumulate quickly. Invest in bins, trays, shelves, and drawers to keep the studio uncluttered. Keep tools and equipment well maintained, organized, in good working order, and in their designated place in their work area. Metals and other materials should also be sorted and separated.

Most metalwork techniques require setup and preparation prior to actually performing the technique. These processes are much easier when specific tools and materials are easily accessible. The setup for a complex soldering joint is easily compromised if the right tool to finish the job cannot be located.

Labeling items in the studio is another key to maintaining organization. Chemicals should always be labeled, especially when small amounts have been transferred out of their original containers. Labeling drawers with a description of their contents will help in finding items that aren't used frequently. Old typesetter's trays have lots of tiny compartments that can be used for sorting metals, findings, materials, and especially beads. Storage trays for other small components are available at hardware and craft stores, too.

TOP Always keep materials well organized. The small compartments of these old wooden printer's trays are ideal for jewelry components and miscellaneous parts.

CENTER Labeling drawers, trays, and bins helps keep your studio organized. A well-organized studio is not only safer, it's more functional.

BOTTOM Old typesetter trays feature tiny compartments for beads, findings, and stones. This tray is filled with coral and turquoise beads.

RIGHT Studio chemicals should be labeled clearly. Always put them back in their proper place when finished. If the brand name labels are too small to read from a distance, or they have fallen off over time, make new labels so there's no guesswork.

Environmental and Safety Concerns

When working with metal, you will be using aggressive chemicals, working with compressed gasses that are highly flammable, and creating dangerous fumes that should not be inhaled. Jeweler's studios are generally safe, however, as long as certain precautions have been met. Safeguard your tools, equipment, and chemicals from children and anyone not familiar with potential dangers. Also advise others that dangerous chemicals, toxic fumes, and risk of fire are potential hazards in the home.

VENTILATION

Because soldering and other heating techniques produce noxious fumes, a good ventilation system is imperative. If your work space is a shared living area, you must consider the risk to others. Even a simple kitchen-style hood that vents to an outside wall will suffice.

One of the more significant health concerns in your studio is air quality. Consider installing a ventilation hood in the work area.

DIY Exhaust Vent

To assemble a simple box-style exhaust vent for your work area, you will need a window near your work area and a small box-style bathroom fan. Most of the supplies can be bought from your neighborhood or big-box hardware store.

Chain large gas and oxygen tanks to a stable, rigid, upright structure, such as your studio wall. Always use flashback arrestors with your regulators, and check your equipment often for leaks.

GAS STORAGE

When storing and using flammable compressed gasses in your home it is important to remember the risk of fire and potential explosion. Always secure large gas and oxygen tanks using a chain to a stable, rigid, upright structure. Your studio wall is ideal. It is never a good idea to store compressed gases in cylindrical tanks in your home. You may need to consult your local fire department for special permits to have these in a residential area. Small, disposable propane and oxygen tanks, also known as plumber's-style tanks, require no permits. Read all warning labels on fuel sources.

CHEMICALS

Chemicals used in jeweler's studios range from slightly harmful to extremely dangerous. As you become more familiar with various processes and advanced techniques, be aware of the chemicals associated with them and their potential dangers. Advanced techniques such as etching use nitric acid, which is much more corrosive than battery acid. Less dangerous alternatives, such as ferric chloride, can be used to etch with limited capabilities. It is the slow-acting chemicals that have a residual effect that are usually the most harmful. Take care to read all instructions and precautions associated with each chemical, and be sure to label and properly store all your chemicals.

SAFETY EQUIPMENT

Most jewelers have never sustained major injuries, but accidents can happen. To avoid potential injury, follow those basic rules of caution.

First, always wear eye protection when performing any technique or process. Do not allow yourself to become content not wearing eye protection. Even if you wear corrective glasses, you should still invest in a good pair of safety glasses.

Second, wear an apron when working. Full-grain cow leather or suede is ideal. Loose-fitting clothing and apron strings can quickly become wound in your bench grinder or buffing wheel, so always tie your apron in the back. An apron will also protect you and your clothing from splashing chemicals, such as pickling solution. Even a tiny splash of solution will leave holes in your clothing after its next wash.

Third, an important addition to your jeweler's studio is a first aid kit. Even if you take every precaution, accidents occur and you may need it.

ABOVE Always wear safety glasses when using a buffing machine. This style of machine has a hood and filter system to minimize the debris that becomes airborne when polishing.

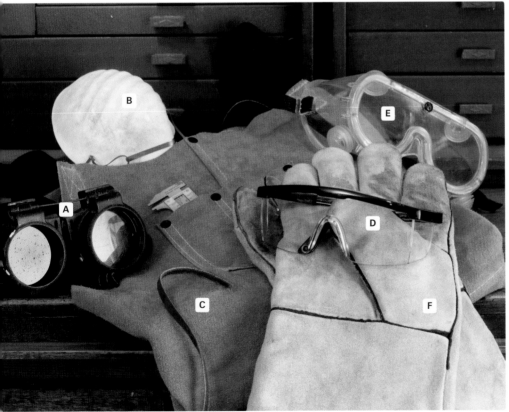

LEFT Studio safety essentials: (A) welder's goggles; (B) dust mask; (C) leather apron; (D) safety glasses; (E) safety goggles; and (F) welder's gloves

Jeweler's
Studio Tools

For techniques as varied as stone setting and forging, jewelers require a variety of specialized tools. Jewelers' tools can be as simple as a mandrel or as advanced as a computer. Most jewelers' tools are simple hand tools, and many studios benefit from a few pieces of equipment, such as a torch set for soldering and a saw for cutting metal. This chapter explores the basics as well as the specialized tools that all well-equipped jewelers' studios should have. From a sturdy workbench to fine drill bits, outfitting the studio should be enjoyable and rewarding.

As with planning your work area, always keep functionality and utility in mind. The work space and its tools establish an environment that can function smoothly while inspiring creative work.

Furnishing Your Studio

As with decorating a home, outfitting the studio with tools and equipment may occur slowly over a period of time, while some jewelers may want to outfit a studio all at once. Whatever your intentions or budget, try to buy the best tools and equipment you can afford. This section will address the basics for outfitting a well-equipped studio. Tools and equipment for specialized processes, such as enameling or casting, can always be added at a later time.

Workbenches

There is a variety of jeweler's-style workbenches commercially available that can be purchased preassembled (or not). Also, sturdy desks and tables can be modified into quality workbenches, or a used workbench can be acquired.

Standard base-model jeweler's benches come with a central area for a bench pin, a few holes for ring mandrels, and a few drawers for organizing tools. When shopping for a jeweler's bench, there are a lot of options. Be sure to get a model with a removable sweeps catch for easier cleanup. If you are considering a serious hobby or even a career in jewelry, opt for the deluxe model. They are usually sturdier, have removable armrests, and are built to last for years.

WATCHMAKER'S BENCH

Watchmaker's benches do not usually have a cutout for a bench pin, and do not have armrests or mandrel holes, but they do have a lot more drawers. If space is a factor, they can prove to be more useful for organizing tools. Some alterations will need to be made to affix a bench pin. Nice watchmaker's, typesetter's, and jeweler's benches can be found at antiques stores or auctions. Some craftspeople feel it is worth paying a premium for an original, solid piece of furniture that is no longer available new.

BENCH PIN

A bench pin is a wedge-shaped block of wood that is affixed to the jeweler's bench. The most popular type is affixed to any table with a C-clamp. Most premade bench pins are relatively inexpensive. Consider purchasing one that already has the V shape cut out of it. Alternatively, a bench pin can be made at home cutting a V shape into 4 × 6 inches (10.2 × 15.2 cm) piece of wood.

DIY Table-to-Workbench Upgrade

Clamp a bench pin in the center of a sturdy, wood table, and a simple, inexpensive jeweler's studio workbench has been created. Staple canvas or suede to the underside of the table to create a sweeps catch. When seated, pull the fabric onto your lap to catch any debris or tools from falling on the floor. (Sweeps catches are especially helpful when working with gemstones.)

Fabric sweeps catch with clamp-style bench pin mounted on a sturdy table

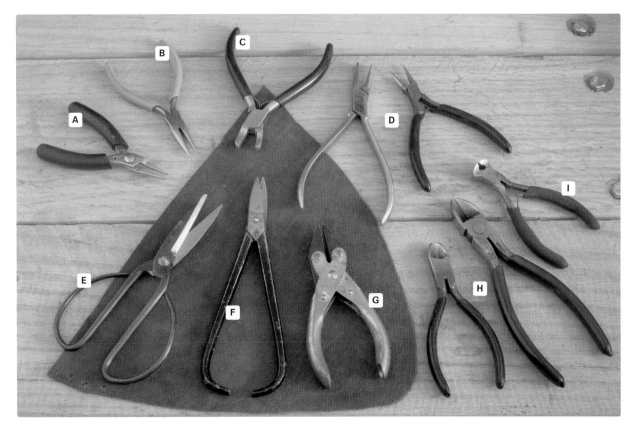

Assortment of hand tools: (A) flat-nosed pliers; (B) chain-nosed pliers; (C) stone-setting pliers; (D) round-nosed pliers; (E) pruning shears; (F) jeweler's snips; (G) parallel-action pliers; (H) small and large flush-side pliers; (I) nippers

Hand Tools

Hand tools are used for holding, shaping, and cutting metals. When considering purchasing hand tools, always buy the best quality tools you can afford. The most expensive brand or style isn't necessary, but be sure that the tools are precision manufactured. Quality tool purchases are an investment in the experience of working with jewelry. Hand tools especially, will prove to be the most used tools in your studio and will get used time and again, so be sure to have the best your money can buy.

PLIERS, NIPPERS, CUTTERS, SCISSORS, AND SHEARS

Pliers come in many different shapes and sizes to serve a number of functions. Most jewelers use four basic shapes of pliers: round nose, flat nose, chain nose, and bent nose. Parallel action pliers are handy, as they compress with equal, parallel force to hold objects. In addition, nylon jaw-type pliers are convenient for holding your work without marring. Some pliers help you with specialized tasks such as prong pushing, prong lifting, stone removing, stone setting, ring holding, and wire working. Once you become more familiar with their intended uses, you may find yourself purchasing a barrage of pliers.

Cross-action hand tools that cut metal are called jeweler's snips or shears. They are used to cut thin sheet metal from templates or to cut tiny squares of sheet solder. Gardening or pruning scissors work as alternatives. The most common type of nipper or cutter is a flush-cut style, which cuts wire without leaving a sharp, pinched point. Bevel-style cutters are great for quick cuts and heavy-gauge wire, but they don't leave a clean cut.

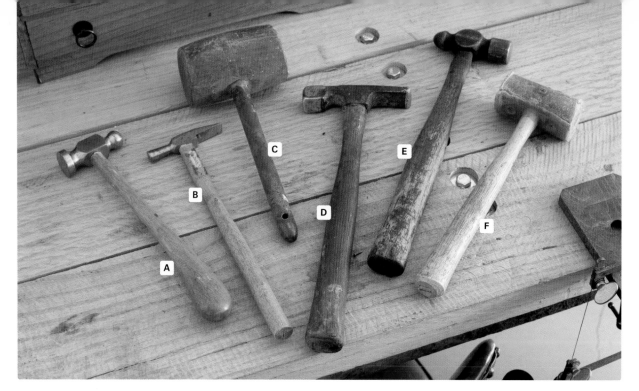

HAMMERS

Hammers are a jeweler's best friend. Used to apply a swift, blunt force to move metal, they serve just as many functions as pliers. Hammers come in a variety of shapes, weights, and sizes, but the three basic types are listed here.

Advanced silversmith and goldsmith hammers should never be used with a tool to strike metals. They also should be kept free of scratches, dents, and imperfections and should be stored either on a wall or separate from one another to prevent damage to the ends. Advanced silversmith and goldsmith hammers come in a few styles used for specific tasks, including raising, creasing, planishing, and embossing. These are the types of hammers that are used to make bowls and cups from flat sheet metal. They usually have highly polished surfaces and are made to balance when held in the hand.

Other styles of hammers include riveting or watchmaker's, which are used to tap small objects or to work in small spaces.

Every studio jeweler should own a rawhide mallet, which is used for moving metal without distorting the surface like steel hammers do. It is great for sizing rings and bending metals without marring.

ABOVE Assortment of hammers: (A) chasing hammer; (B) riveting or watchmaker's hammer; (C) wooden mallet; (D) bricklayer's hammer; (E) ball-peen hammer; and (F) rawhide mallet. If shaped and polished with a little modification, a brick- layer's hammer can be a great creasing or raising hammer.

BELOW A silversmith's hammer is a very balanced hammer. It is always highly polished to minimize the transfer of non-desirable texture to the surface of a metal. These tools should always be cared for properly and protected against unnecessary wear.

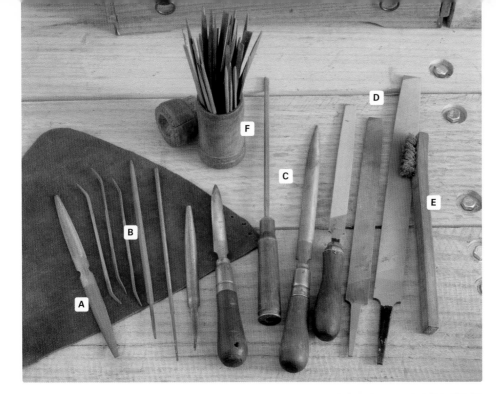

LEFT Assortment of files: (A) wax carving file; (B) escapement and riffler-style files; (C) round, square, and half-round files with and without handles; (D) flat files; (E) brass wire-bristle brush for cleaning files; (F) needle files in assorted shapes.

BELOW Various holding devices: (A) tubing cutter jig; (B) hand vice with parallel jaws; (C) wooden clamp-style ring holder with leather insert and wooden wedge; (D) pin-style hand vice

FILES

Files are used to remove large amounts of metal during each pass. For most applications use the largest file you are comfortable with. The three basic shapes of files are flat, half round, and full round, which come in many degrees of cuts. Files are numbered from zero (coarse cut) to as high as six (very fine cut).

Needle files are miniature versions of the large files. They are graded the same way and come in a variety of shapes and degrees of cuts. Shapes of needle files include square, barrette, crossed, equaling, half round, knife, triangle, and three square. Needle files are usually sold as a set, which will include all the basic shapes you will need for jewelry work.

Escapement files are used against surfaces that you do not want scratched, and riffler files are bent for working in hard-to-reach areas.

Store your files so they do not touch. If they are banging around against one another, they will dull. Always file in one direction and never drag the tool backwards across the surface, which will also dull your files. Use a brass bristle brush to clean the teeth of your files. Also, never allow your files to get wet, as they will rust quickly. It is possible to set your files in handles, although most jewelers don't.

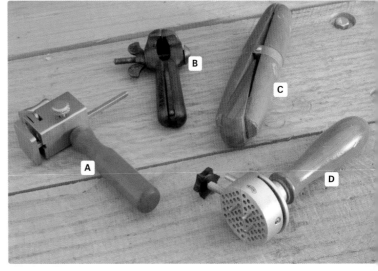

HOLDING TOOLS

Miniature clamps and hand vices are perfect for holding small pieces of jewelry while you apply pressure with tools. Another holding tool is a ring clamp, which is usually wooden and designed with leather jaws that hold your work firmly when the wedge is inserted. Wooden ring clamps are an essential beginner's tool. You can use them to hold rings while you set stones or to hold your work while polishing. These holding devices are often called setting tools.

LEFT Stone-setting and engraving tools: (A) wooden handles; (B) bead-setting tool set; (C) crocker-style graver sharpener with Arkansas stone and tool oil can; (D) double-sided sharpening stone, and leather strips; (E) gravers not yet set in handles; (F) millegrain tool; (G) miniature hand chuck; (H) two gravers with the cutting ends protected by cork

OPPOSITE An array of forming and stamping tools: (A) doming block and punches set; (B) stamping set; (C) number and letter stamping set; (D) railroad bolt; (E) brass dapping block; (F) center punch; (G) bent stamps; (H) miscellaneous punches; (I) lead block; and (J) disc-cutting tool.

BELOW From left to right: thin, tapered mandrel used to shape and form bezel and wire, square steel rod used for making angles, Slotted and smooth ring mandrels. Front: bracelet mandrel inserted in steel bench block vice clamped to a sturdy workbench ready for hammering

SETTING TOOLS

Setting tools are generally grouped not by the style of tool but by purpose. Considered an advanced tool group, they are used to set objects, including faceted gemstones, cabochon semiprecious stones, or beads, in different metal holding devices such as prongs, bezels, or pins.

The burnishing tool, in either straight or slightly curved styles, is a polished steel tool used to smooth metal around the lip of a stone after bezel setting.

A bezel roller is used for rolling metal around the outer lip of a stone by means of a rocking motion. This steel tool usually comes with a wooden handle.

A bezel pusher, another polished steel tool with a wooden handle, is typically a square shank tool used for pushing metal bezel with force to pinch the stone in place.

These three tools, although inexpensive, can be made yourself. Many times jewelers will modify other tools or make their own tool for a specific task by using other pieces of tool steel such as broken files or burrs.

MANDRELS

Square mandrels are used to shape metal into crisp corners. Ring mandrels are used to shape and even-size rings. Jewelers use ring mandrels in conjunction with a rawhide mallet to size up rings a quarter or half size. Sizing up a ring more than one full size requires soldering.

Forming Tools

Forming tools are used to bend and shape metal. These tools are primarily made from polished tool-grade steel, though brass, wooden, and other models are available as well. The simplest forming tools are forming blocks or dapping blocks. The tops of these blocks feature cavities into which the metal is pushed or hammered, using dapping punches, to create the shapes desired. The dapping block creates curved, hemispheric shapes and the forming block creates grooved, bent, or tube-style shapes.

Another great addition to any jeweler's toolbox is the disc-cutting tool. It cuts precise equal-size discs from sheet metals. Insert sheet metal into the hole of choice, and then insert the cutting punch. With a swift blow from a heavy mallet, the tool will produce small round discs of various sizes. Discs pair well with the dapping block and punches set.

Domes are used as a resist shape for forming metal. They are used in conjunction with hammers to create the shape. An egg-shaped dome is used to create a spoon shape and a round dome can be used to create a bowl shape.

Other forming tools include hand stamps, lettering stamps, and chasing tools.

Nontraditional Forming Tools

Obscure objects, such as huge steel bolts from old buildings or bridges, railroad nails, and sections of railroad track, are often found in well-appointed jewelers' studios. All of these make excellent forming tools, augmenting a typical collection of domes, blocks, and punches.

Have fun while experimenting with novel objects and play with their forming potential. While wearing eye and hand protection, clean the rust away from the work surface with a harsh abrasive to reveal bright, fresh steel. Then file, sand, and polish the surface to a mirror finish.

Railroad track has a combination of nontraditional uses in the studio. It has a nice, crisp corner on one side and a soft, smooth curve on the other, both of which are perfect for forming metal. It doubles as a bench block for hammering or riveting.

Railroad nail heads are a wonderful forming tool. They take the shape of a perfect spoon when used with silversmith hammers. Railroad nails and large steel bolts serve best when secured in a vice.

Basic Studio Equipment

Once you have amassed all of the hand tools needed for basic fabrication, a few benchtop pieces of equipment can round out your jewelry-making studio. Most jewelers' studios have the following:

FLEXIBLE-SHAFT TOOL

Using specific bits with a flexible-shaft tool, you can drill, grind, sand, polish, and shape metal to prepare for stone setting. Most fine bench jewelers use the flexible-shaft tool with a variety of setting burrs to set all types of faced stones.

This rotary-style tool usually comes with a hanging motor, foot pedal, hand piece, and long flexible shaft. The motor should be mounted on a swinging hook or its own mast. The motor will twist and move about depending on the speed and torque of the application.

The motor should be suspended high enough to allow you to use the tool above, below, and all around the area of the bench pin. Suspend the motor low enough so that the flexible shaft will allow you to use the hand piece at any angle and with either hand. The convenient foot pedal allows you to control the speed of the tool from a super-slow rotation all the way up to full power.

Some techniques require a half or one full rotation of the shaft, which cannot be achieved with a Dremel-style tool. The biggest advantage of a flexible-shaft tool is the availability of hand pieces, which are interchangeable and can be swapped out quickly. A hammer attachment is handy, but the standard hand piece is the adjustable chuck, which can accommodate any size drill bit or attachment.

Flexible-shaft tool suite: (A) Adjustable chuck hand piece with key (in mini vise); (B) motor and an assortment of finishing bits with polishing compound; (C) various muslin and felt buffs; (D) bristle, wire, and rubber wheels; (E) sanding split shaft and disc

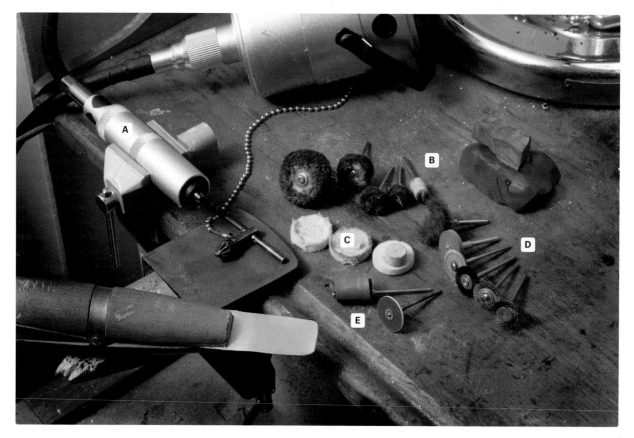

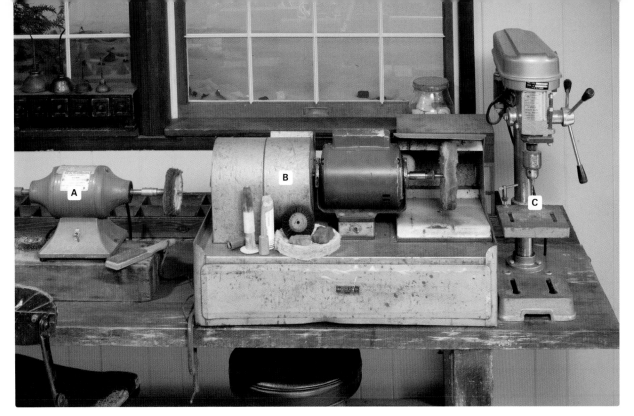

(A) Benchtop tools: Single-phase buffing lathe with tapered spindles and muslin buffs; (B) metal polishing cabinet with hood, filter, dust collector, single-phase motor, tapered spindle, and muslin buff; (C) benchtop drill press

DRILL PRESS

A small benchtop drill press allows you to secure your work and drill repeated precise holes with great control. This is sometimes necessary when drilling different parts that later need to be attached with rivets, screws, or pins. Like the flexible-shaft tool, you can outfit your drill press with a variety of different bits. A drill press is great for drilling with diamond-coated bits into glass or ceramic. It is helpful to be able to control the downward pressure by gently pressing the bit into the secured work. Buy a model with an adjustable table and a keyless chuck.

BUFFER/POLISHING LATHE

Sometimes this tool is referred to as a buffing cabinet, which is because most models come with a dust collector hood. These styles are ideal because they collect and filter the air from dust particles that contain metal and polishing compounds. These cabinet styles come with either one or two shafts. If you can afford to purchase the two-shaft style, it makes for easier finishing and polishing without the need for changing out buffs. Use a benchtop motor style without the hood or filter for occasional use.

All buffing lathes can be outfitted with tapered spindles. They are tapered and threaded, either on the right or left side, in order to change out buffs quickly without hardware.

A single muslin or felt buff should be dedicated to a specific compound, such as Tripoli. Change your buff when changing to a different polishing compound such as rouge, so keep a box or drawer near for storing your various buffing wheels.

Your polishing setup can be as simple as a ¼ hp motor attached to your workbench with one tapered spindle or can be as elaborate as a whole studio dust filtration system equipped with air purifiers. Some other attachments for your buffing machine include wood sanding mandrels, ring buffing mandrels, abrasive sleeves, and laps.

BENCHTOP GRINDER

Another lathe-style motorized tool, the bench grinder is available in a full-power, high-speed style or in a smaller version with an adjustable speed dial, the latter of which is adequate for a jeweler's studio. There are even ones that can have a flexible-shaft tool attached.

Bench grinders are great for heavy-duty work that may stress your hand tools. They are ideal for working with various hard materials and quickly take off large amounts of material. Always install and use the supplied tool rests and shields. Use caution when grinding, keeping your fingers clear of the stone.

Most jewelers will make a few of their own hand tools, most of which are shaped using a bench grinder. A few multiuse grinders come with a wet stone option. Grinding with water irrigates and lubricates most materials and prevents overheating. Advanced wet stone grinders are used by lapidary shops to cut, shape, and polish precious gemstones.

ROLLING MILL

Every jeweler's studio should have a rolling mill, which is used to reduce or flatten sheet metal. This is done by a series of passes through the mill, each time gradually increasing the pressure. Rolling mills can accept sheet metal as thick as a stick of gum and roll it out thinner than tissue paper. The rolling mill uses gears to create the force needed to stretch metal to its limits. The tool is designed to transfer power to the rollers with minimal effort while turning the large handle.

Rolling mills can also be used to reduce wire and ring stock. They come with combination rollers that make sheet metal, round wire, and half round wire. You can buy textured rollers that make all sorts of different patterns on your metal or you can experiment by inserting various screening, fabric, and other materials along with the sheet metal when it is passed through the mill. The outcome of textures and patterns is always surprising. Many jewelers use rolling mills to fabricate their own stock. This practice involves melting your scrap metal, pouring an ingot, and rolling out your own sheet metals and wire.

SHEAR

A shear, a steel benchtop tool that complements the rolling mill, is designed to cut sheet metals up to 14-gauge thick. Sheet metal is inserted into the shear and aligned with the cutting blade. A large lever is used to transfer the force to the cutting edge. The shear makes precise, straight cuts that are often difficult to achieve with a jeweler's saw. In conjunction with the rolling mill, a sheet metal shear is used to cut strips of various gauges of metal, or to make plumb, measured square edges on larger pieces. The tool usually has a combination feature that bends metal at 90- and 45-degree angles. Using the tool's lever, sheet metal is inserted and bent with the same action as cutting. The shear makes quick folds, cuts, and edges in your metals.

Soldering Equipment

Set up a soldering station, either as part of your workbench or separately, away from chemicals and objects. A station also allows you to vent soldering fumes with a hood. Basic soldering equipment includes:

TORCHES

A handheld "mini" torch set (not a plumber's-style torch) is recommended because it allows the user to control the flame and oxygen flow. They can be fitted to disposable tanks available at your local hardware store. This style torch set is recommended for beginners and those who do not want large fuel and oxygen cylinders in the home. They have interchangeable tips, depending on the task at hand. Choose a medium tip until you become more familiar with tips and their intended uses.

SOLDERING SURFACE

An old kiln firebrick or ceramic pads, available at most jeweler's suppliers, work as soldering surfaces. Charcoal bricks can be used as well, but they deteriorate easily and break down faster than ceramic.

A newer material, carbon fiber, acts as a blanket

Torch assortment: (A) canister-style oxy-propane set with mini-torch hand piece; (B) butane torch; (C) large casting torch with rosette-style tip; (D) striker and midget-style torch heads. The mini-torch has a variety of tip choices for flames.

because it is fireproof and creates a solid heat barrier. This fiber material is sometimes used to line a workbench surface to protect from heat and reduce the risk of fire. Always plan your workstation with safety in mind. Never set up soldering equipment near flammable items like lamp shades, paperwork, or chemicals.

SOLDERING TOOLS

A soldering pick, usually made of titanium, allows you to work your solder and assists with picking up solder pieces. Soldering tweezers come in a straight or bent-tip style. Choose counterlocking styles that have an insulated handle. You will also need cool water nearby. A jar or bowl will do, but a stainless steel sink is ideal.

FLUX

Flux is the solution applied to the surface of your work to aid in the flow of solder. It cleans and protects the metal and solder from the dirty oxides in the torch flame. During the soldering process, oxides build up on the surface of your work and cause the solder not to flow. Flux is designed to keep the surface of your solder joint clean and withstand the flame.

Although there are different kinds of flux used for different materials, the flux most used for soldering gold is called Batterns flux, which is a clear yellow fluid that paints on easily. The most basic form of flux is borax. It is sold in a solid cone form that is then ground and mixed with water. There are commercially available fluxes that have a premixed combination of borax and other ingredients. Handy flux is a thick paste-like substance that works well with many different metals and techniques.

PICKLE

Pickle is a solution used to clean metal when finished soldering. Cooled flux on the surface of your work is hard like glass. The corrosive nature of pickle removes the flux residue and the oxides created from soldering.

Jewelers once used a dangerous mixture of sulfuric acid and water but a safer, friendlier solution is Sparex No. 2, a dry granular powder that contains sodium bisulfate. It still presents a marginal health risk but is much safer than acid. Follow the instructions for correct mixture of solution to water.

Pickle is best used warm. There are specific electric pickle pots for this purpose, but a small slow cooker works great. Always use copper tongs when placing your work in the pickle. A chemical reaction similar to plating happens with steel tools. Be sure to not splash the pickle solution on your clothes, it will make holes after the next wash. Always rinse your work after removing from the pickle and wash your hands. Discard your pickle after it loses effectiveness or begins to turn bluish green, and always neutralize your pickle with baking soda before discarding.

STATION SETUP

Much of soldering involves setting up for the task and preparing your piece to be soldered. A few last items to have on hand include a spool of binding wire (used to bind objects for soldering), a third hand (a set of tweezers affixed to a heavy metal base), a soldering tripod (used to elevate your work piece and allow torch heat underneath), and stabilizing pins (used to push into your firebrick or charcoal block to stabilize your work).

Advanced Equipment

The options for advanced equipment are vast, but advanced equipment should consist of items that will make you more efficient. Usually these types of tools are the beginning of production-based work. Over time you may want to begin to duplicate your items, produce runs of more than one piece, or attempt specialized techniques—all of which need advanced equipment.

CASTING EQUIPMENT

Casting is by far the largest collection of various pieces of equipment that you will need to advance your jewelry career. At some point, you will desire to create various shapes, designs, or parts that cannot be made from sheet metal or wire.

Tools and equipment needed for casting are diverse; there are many ways to cast molten metal into shapes. The most basic casting techniques may be in sand, charcoal, or cuttlefish bone. Sling casting is somewhat dangerous, vacuum casting requires specialized vacuum machines, but the easiest to master though is the centrifugal technique. It requires the least amount of expensive equipment and still produces precise castings.

The centrifugal technique requires a kiln (also handy for enameling or firing precious metal clay). The kiln is used to burn out wax models that are encased in investment plaster. Kilns heat a metal flask containing the investment and the wax model which has a sprue attached to a rubber base that will form the inlet hole for the molten metal. During the burnout process, the wax and sprue are evaporated by the high temperature. The casting process is generally complex and should be taught to you by a professional.

The size of the kiln depends on what you intend to use it for. If you are planning on creating a single casting or a number of small castings, you do not need a large capacity kiln. Something in the area of $10 \times 10 \times 8$ feet ($25.4 \times 25.4 \times 20.3$ cm) high internal dimensions will do. A standard firebrick style will do. Be sure to buy one with a pyrometer or optional thermocouple controller. Kilns should always be used in a ventilated area, so consider installing a vent hood or duct fan even for occasional use. Advanced fume hoods should be used if casting on a regular basis.

The main piece of equipment for this casting technique is the easy-to-use centrifugal machine. Once a hot flask is placed in the device, it uses centrifugal energy while spinning to force the molten metal into the cavity. It must be bolted to a sturdy table and is wound up with a heavy spring. Once wound, you can lock the handle to prepare your metal. It has a melting crucible and balance weights inside the safety ring.

Insert the flask from the kiln using tongs while melting your metal in the crucible. Once ready, release the lock to throw the machine into a spinning motion. The metal is flung from the crucible outward into the cavity of the flask filling the shape left from your wax model. After a quick cooling in cold water, your cast piece is freed from the investment.

You will need a few other tools and materials to outfit your casting suites, including investment powder, mixing bowls, measuring containers, scales, investment vibrator or vacuum, flasks, stir rod, casting torch or metal melting furnace, and various other advanced equipment pieces.

Along with outfitting your studio with casting equipment, you will need some simple hand tools designed to carve wax. Special files, burrs, and carving tools are designed to shape wax effectively using traditional techniques. Wax is sold by the block, sheet, or strip and can be worked with warm tools to add or remove areas depending on your design. These wax models can be intricate and complex. When submersed in investment, details as delicate as fingerprints are transferred to the design once created in metal. Wax carving is a learned technique, an acquired skill that takes years to master.

DUPLICATION EQUIPMENT

Once you have learned the basics of casting a model, you may want to duplicate it. You might just need the second identical piece for the other earring or create hundreds of your one design to sell.

The principle behind duplication involves making a mold. This mold can be used to create a single replica or hundreds. Mold making takes a few pieces of specialized equipment. The main tool is a vulcanizer, which is similar to a heated bench press. Metal model and various rubber material is layered into a metal frame, which is then heated and compressed in the vulcanizer to form a solid rubber block. Once cooled, the solid rubber block containing the metal model serves as the basis for duplication.

You start by removing the metal model from inside the rubber block by cutting the block with a razor horizontally starting at the sprue. From there, the block is nearly cut in two. The metal model is removed leaving the impression ready to accept warm wax in its place.

Part of the duplication process involves making numerous identical wax models of the original metal model. This is done with another advanced piece of equipment: the wax injector. It melts wax pellets and scrap to a hot, fluid liquid in a pot. It is a pressurized device that injects the liquid wax into the rubber mold being held with hands. Once cooled, the hardened wax model is removed from the rubber mold allowing it to be used again for the second and third models. This process can be repeated for as many models as needed. These wax models are then set in investment and cast the same way individual hand-carved wax models are cast.

OTHER ADVANCED EQUIPMENT

Advanced equipment depends on where your interests lie. One of the more interesting metals techniques is enameling. This advanced technique uses basic metals skills to introduce color to your designs. Enameling can be learned by trial and error and really only requires the use of a kiln. If you have already set up your studio for casting, then you will already have the basic tools needed for enameling. With the purchase of some various colored enameling powders, you can begin to incorporate color other than gemstones into your work.

Another piece of advanced equipment is a bench press. A press can be used for die-forming metals and other techniques. Die-forming involves transforming sheet metal into three-dimensional shapes by pushing and stretching.

Optional Equipment

Jewelers can incorporate a wide variety of techniques and materials into their work, some of which require even more equipment. Unless you have an interest in using a specific material in your designs, you should not have the need for additional equipment. But if you do fancy, say, beautiful colored gemstones, and you want to cut them yourself from raw material, you would need lapidary equipment.

It is recommended to separate areas of your studio for different interests. Lapidary work, for instance, is very messy. It involves the use of water to cut and grind stones. Many jewelers have basic wet grinders to cut, grind, and polish simple cabochon stones to set in their jewelry designs. But unless you have an interest in cutting your own gemstones, leave it to the lapidary folks.

Another trend in jewelry design is the use of plastics, wood, and other materials, which will be discussed in other chapters. If you have an interest, you can incorporate woodworking equipment into your studio. Even simple scroll saws and belt sanders used for intricate woodworking are handy in any jeweler's studio.

Artist: Grace Chin
Title: *Oval Assemblage Necklace*
Materials: sterling silver, fresh-
water pearls
Techniques: Cast, fabricated

Metal and
Other Materials

Once your studio has been outfitted with all the tools necessary to cut, shape, and join metal, learning and honing the techniques to work with metal is the next step. This chapter covers the basic properties of metal; the fundamentals of metals techniques and processes; and explores the properties of other materials as well. The more knowledge a jeweler has with his or her materials, the more creative they can be with their work. Those who take the time to learn about their material, its limits, and its capabilities are usually the pioneers of great designs.

Properties of Metal

A studio jeweler is by nature a metalsmith. Although most jewelers steer clear of iron and steel, they still are required to be informed about properties of all metals. When working with metal as the primary material, it is helpful to know about a variety of types.

Jewelers historically have worked in nonferrous metals (metals that do not contain iron), which include precious metals and base metals. Gold, silver, and platinum are considered precious metals. Copper, aluminum, brass, nickel, and titanium are base metals. Alloys are mixtures of nonferrous metals that when combined make a new metal, such as bronze. Alloys are generally created for strength or color advantages. Some popular alloys include white gold, rose gold, and sterling silver.

Other alloys include solders; they have various other metals added to silver or gold to reduce the melting points. Some of the metals alloyed to make solder include zinc and cadmium. Depending on the mixtures of the alloy, different grades of solders are created with graduated melting and flow points.

Melting and Flowing Temperatures of Solder

Type	Melt Point	Flow Point
Easy	1260°F (682°C)	1325°F (718°C)
Medium	1335°F (724°C)	1390°F (754°C)
Hard	1435°F (780°C)	1450°F (788°C)

SOLDERS

If you are working on a complex piece of jewelry, always start with hard solder then move to medium for your second solder joint so the previous joint does not reflow. The specific flow temperatures are for technical purposes; most jewelers do not have a way to measure the temperature of their solder before they know when it will flow. This knowledge comes from practice and determining the color of your metal and the heating stage of your flux.

The melting temperatures can range from very low, which is usually labeled "easy" solder, up to middle melting temperatures associated with the "medium" solder, and a much higher temperature named "hard" solder.

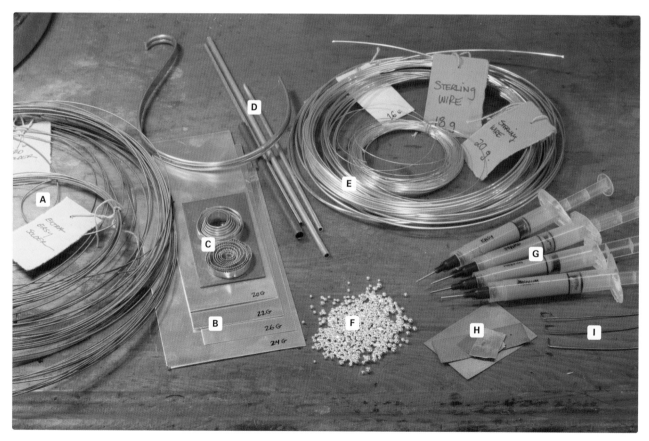

An array of solder and metals: (A) wire solder; (B) sterling and copper sheet metal; (C) fine silver bezel wire; (D) a variety of tubing style; (E) sterling gauge wire; (F) sterling silver casting grain; (G) paste-style solders; (H) sheet-style solders; (I) hard, medium, and easy solder bends

Artist: Timothy Lazure
Title: *Untitled Ring*
Materials: Sterling, 18-karat gold
Techniques: Soldered, fabricated

METAL TYPES

The most common metals in the jewelry studio are precious, although precious metals in their natural state are either too soft or not durable enough to make jewelry suitable for everyday wearing. The most common alloys are related to gold and silver. Silver is alloyed with copper to create sterling, which is harder than silver alone. Sterling is usually stamped so or with a .925 mark to denote nine hundred twenty-five parts per thousand of silver content. The other seventy-five is the copper content. This is the universal unit of measure for most metals. They are graded on a scale of parts per thousand.

> **TIP** | **What Is a Karat?**
>
> The word *karat* is a unit of measure applicable in the United States. For other countries the standard for precious metals is units of measure in parts per one thousand. For instance, 24-karat gold is in the purest form, this would be 1,000 parts per 1,000. Continuing with this scale, 18-karat gold would be 75 percent gold or 750 parts per 1,000.

Artist: Brandon Holschuh
Title: *Telephony*
Materials: Reclaimed phone magnet
housing, resin, seed pods, steel,
copper, glass, sterling
Techniques: Riveted, forged, cold
connected, soldered, fabricated, cast

All of the projects and techniques taught in this book can be used with sterling or gold. As you begin to experiment with other precious metals, it is recommended you learn about each of their specific properties before using them in your work. For instance, aluminum and pewter are contaminants. Residue on your tools from working with these metals will create unwanted reactions when switching back to sterling or gold. Be sure to use separate tools and clean up your work area to avoid contamination. It is considered safe to work with copper, brass, and silver in conjunction with one another. Most jewelers keep separate tools for gold and platinum though.

Some of the most common metals used by studio jewelers are:

PLATINUM

Platinum is a gray-white metal. It is considered the most precious of all the precious metals family. It has a high specific gravity making it one of the heaviest metals. Its superior durability and demand make it the ideal choice for jewelers and buyers. This demand coupled with its superior capabilities make it the most expensive material to work with. Fine jewelry containing very expensive precious gemstones is usually crafted from platinum. It has a unique property that allows it to hold its luster and avoid tarnishing and scratches.

Platinum is expensive, is not easy to work with, and usually requires its own tools, polishing compounds, and specialized equipment. Due to its very high melting temperature, it is not able to be cast with standard casting methods. Most studio jewelers do not cast their own platinum, nor do they work with it in traditional shapes such as wire and sheet forms.

GOLD

Pure gold is a rich yellow, malleable, soft metal. Its natural ability to resist corrosion and tarnish make it by far the most workable of all the precious metals. Because gold in its purest form is much too soft for making jewelry, it is almost always alloyed with other metals to harden it. These alloys can also be mixed to create colors such as white, red, and green. For beginner jewelers, gold is easier to learn to solder than any other metal. Silversmiths and goldsmiths share the same tools and equipment due to the similar working properties of the metals. Market price fluctuations on gold make it a reliable investment as well as enjoyed by the wearer as a rich, luxurious material.

SILVER

Silver is white metal that in its natural form is almost as soft and malleable as gold. Silver has a natural ability to resist corrosion, but it will tarnish when exposed to the environment. Anyone who as ever owned a sterling flatware set can attest that silver tarnishes naturally. Silver alone is able to be worked and worn as jewelry, but it is commonly alloyed with copper to harden it. This alloy is called sterling silver. Sterling silver is a little more difficult to solder than gold, but most craftspeople make easy use of it. Due to its easy working properties, ability to hold a luster, and beautiful reflective properties, sterling is the material of choice among studio jewelers. It is also the least expensive of all the precious metals family. Silver is also available in the most forms (sheets, strips, wires, and grains).

COPPER

Copper is a red metal. In its purest form, it is a very soft and malleable material that tarnishes easily and patinas fast. It has high sulfur content that when exposed to environmental agents produces the rich blue-green patina. Copper is a relatively inexpensive metal and is ideal for use as a practice material to learn soldering and other metals techniques, including raising. It has a high melting temperature and can be sawn, filed, and polished with the same tools as silver. When used appropriately, copper can add a rich design element to jewelry. Most copper jewelry is coated with a protective layer to prevent staining the wearer's skin green or is lined with sterling where it will make contact with skin. Copper can be hammered, work hardened, and annealed quite nicely.

BRASS

Brass is an alloy composed of copper and zinc. It is not corrosive but tarnishes easily. It patinas fast due to the high copper content. Brass is an inexpensive learning material. It has a relatively low melting temperature, so use caution when attempting to solder with it.

BRONZE

Bronze is an alloy composed of copper and tin. It is an inexpensive alloy that tarnishes and patinas quite beautifully over time. It has been used by sculptors and metalsmiths for centuries due to its durability and multitude of uses. It is the metal of choice for model makers and casters. Studio jewelers often use it to practice casting.

NICKEL SILVER

Contrary to its name, nickel silver contains no silver. It is named so due to the fact that it is a white metal that appears similar to silver. Its alloy consists of copper, nickel, and zinc. It is difficult to work with and solder and it can irritate the wearer's skin. Quite a few people have sensitivity to nickel silver. Nickel silver is generally used for practice drilling and sawing.

Selecting Metal

One of the most intimidating and challenging tasks for jewelers is buying metals. Metals are manufactured in a variety of shapes, sizes, thicknesses, and lengths. All of these forms are associated with some unit of measure. Making matters worse, units of measure vary from country to country and from supplier to supplier. Units of measure may include metric, inch fractions, or scales.

The most common unit of measure is Brown and Sharpe, or the B&S. The B&S system is used to indicate a metal's thickness and is commonly used as the unit of measure when buying sheet metal and round wire. B&S is confusing for the beginner because the unit of measure is reversed from standard units of measure. The higher the B&S number the thinner the

Brown and Sharpe Gauge

Brown & Sharpe Gauge	Inches	Millimeters
2	0.257	6.52
4	0.204	5.18
6	0.162	4.11
8	0.128	3.24
10	0.101	2.57
12	0.080	2.03
14	0.064	1.63
16	0.050	1.27
18	0.040	1.02
20	0.031	0.79
22	0.025	0.64
24	0.020	0.51
26	0.015	0.38
28	0.012	0.30
30	0.010	0.25

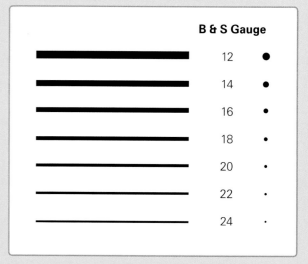

It is recommended that you purchase an inexpensive handheld gauge to help you decide what gauge metals to order.

metal. A low B&S number, say 2 or 4, is a very heavy, thick piece of metal. Even though the chart shown indicates the B&S number as it corresponds to inches and millimeters, it is always difficult to visualize how the metal will look once you order it.

When ordering sheet metal, it is common to order by dimensions. Sheet metal comes in 6 or 12 inches (15.2 or 30.5 cm) widths in all gauges. It is usually sold by the inch, meaning if you wanted only 1 inch (2.5 cm) of the 6 inch (15.2 cm)-wide style in a 16-gauge thickness, then your piece would be sold to you as a 1 × 6 inch (2.5 × 15.2 cm) strip, about the size of a bracelet, once shaped.

Because the price is set by weight, your 1 × 6 inch (2.5 × 15.2 cm) piece is then weighed and priced by the troy ounce. The process is made easier by ordering the smallest quantity available and keeping those examples as a reference until you become more familiar with the ordering process. If you have a local jeweler's supplier, where you are able to handle the metals, shop there first.

When ordering wire, first decide on the shape. Wire comes in different shapes, including round, flat, square, half round, oval, and triangle. If you decide that round wire is what you need, you must next decide the gauge. Using your sheet and wire gauge is helpful to identify the B&S number. Wire is also sold by the inch. Most suppliers will only sell a minimum of 12 inch (30.5 cm) of any wire higher than 18 gauge. Determine the length, in increments of 12 inch (30.5 cm). When ordering, you would say: "(type) sterling silver wire, (style) round, (thickness) 18 gauge, (length) 50 inches." The wire is dispensed, and then weighed for a daily calculated market price. All metals are sold by this system with the exception of casting grain, which is sold by weight. You can order any kind of metal this way, although silver and gold offer the most styles and choices.

Other styles of metal available from most suppliers include tubing, bezel, and ring stock. These styles are sold similarly to sheet and wire but do not use the B&S gauge system. They are sold by a combination of millimeters to identify the dimensions and again sold by the inch.

ANNEALING AND HARDENING METAL

Each type of metal has its own unique properties that significantly differ from metal to metal. The metal properties are varied even more by the alloying process. It is sometimes necessary to become familiar with one particular metal, to know it intimately, and work with it independently. Most craftspeople first work with sterling silver due to its relatively low cost.

Metals change molecular structure when stretched, hammered, bent, or heated. Any action where metal changes its shape is called work hardening. Sterling is a relatively malleable metal in its dormant state. Once worked even just slightly, it becomes "half hard." If you continue to push, stretch, or move the metal further it is called "hard." If you continue working the metal even further to nearly its breaking point, it is "spring hard." It is just past this last stage where your metal will begin to crack, flake, and chip as it begins to break down.

The process of reversing this action is called annealing, which involves torch-heating your metal to a barely visible red (1100°F to 1150°F [593°C to 621°C] for sterling silver). This heating of your metal restores the molecular composition back to a malleable state. From there, you can continue working with it without risk of damage. Each time you solder, at every step, your work is annealed. If you are working with a piece that does not require soldering, be sure to anneal every so often.

TIP Annealing Your Metal

When sterling reaches an annealing temperature of 1100°F to 1150°F (593°C to 621°C), it becomes dull red. Hold it there for a few seconds then quickly remove the heat, and quench in water. By continuing to heat after this point you risk raising the temperature to sterling's melting point of 1640°F (893°C). If the metal changes from dull red to bright cherry red, your metal is about to melt.

MAKING YOUR OWN METAL STOCK

Many studio jewelers make their own sheet metal and wire. Making your own stock is fairly simple and requires only a few basic tools; however, the process is long and time-consuming, and it requires dedication to the craft. Some jewelers do it because they like to control the alloy and add more or less gold content. Some do it to save on cost, recycling their scrap into new sheet and wire. Some do it for ethical reasons that will slow down the mining of precious metals and the environmental impact. Whatever the reason, making your own stock is a rewarding experience.

First, decide what metals you wish to recycle, which can include broken chains, bent rings, even scrap cuttings from your projects. Remove any clasps, soldered areas, and other contaminants. Place the items in a melting crucible, heat until flowing, then pour the molten metal into ingot molds. The shapes of these molds vary depending on the style of the ingot. Most ingots are flat bars for making sheet, or thick sticks for making wire. Be sure to heat your mold in conjunction with your metal. Pouring molten metal into a cold mold is a recipe for disaster.

Once cooled, the metal is removed from the mold and the process of hammering, rolling, and stretching begins. As the metal is flattened in the rolling mill it becomes work hardened, so a large portion of the process is devoted to annealing. After every second or third pass through the rolling mill, your piece will need to be annealed, quenched, and dried; the beginning process is then repeated.

Wire is made the same way, but along with a rolling mill it is pulled through a drawplate, a thick steel plate that is secured in a bench-top vice. The plate contains a series of holes, from very large to very small. The process is started by passing your stick ingot through a rolling mill and reducing it through the series of grooves in the mill's roller. Once it cannot be reduced any further in the mill, it is transferred to the drawplate. By starting with the largest hole, the wire is passed through each hole consecutively. This process of passing the wire through the holes repeatedly is called drawing. Drawing down or reducing

your wire is time-consuming. Every few passes you must anneal, quench, dry, and repeat the beginning process. The process uses draw tongs to hold onto the end of the wire as it is pulled through the holes. It is a good idea to lubricate the wire with a bit of beeswax for smooth pulling action.

Soldering Process

Once you have familiarized yourself with metal types, their properties, and how they are sold, you need to learn to work with them. The single most important technique that studio jewelers need to master is soldering. Soldering is the act of permanently joining two ends of metal together using heat and solder.

> ### TIP | Torch Tip
>
> Always turn off the oxygen valve first, then the gas; otherwise, a whip-crack sound will happen as the oxygen overtakes the torch flame.

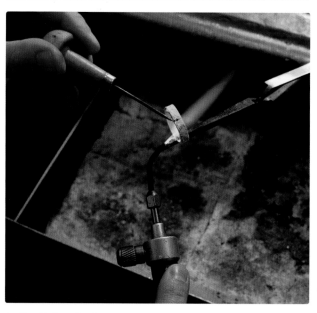

In chip soldering, using the transfer method, chips of solder are balled up with the flame then transferred to the joint using a pick.

BASIC TECHNIQUE:
Soldering

There are three basic techniques for soldering: stick, chip, and paste. The technique most taught and easiest to learn is chip soldering, shown here.

This is where small squares of solder are cut from a sheet. The "chips" are transferred to the solder joint using tweezers or a soldering pick and the object is heated until the solder flows. The sheet solders can be purchased in a hard, medium, or easy grade, hardest being the highest melting point and easy being the lowest melting point. Soldering requires the use of a torch and a few other tools and chemicals, all of which were covered in chapter 2, page 22. It is a technique most easily mastered with practice, so don't be discouraged. Review torches and torch safety before attempting any soldering technique.

SOLDERING PREPARATION

Soldering is all about preparation, which starts with good-fitting joints. Other factors include stabilizing your work with pins or binding wire to ensure nothing moves while you are soldering. Preparation includes the right amount of solder, and the cleanliness of your metals and solder. A good way to clean dirt and oils from your work before soldering is to immerse it in pickle solution, which will clean the dirt and oils that transfer from your skin. Be sure to rinse and dry before soldering.

To light your torch, use a torch lighter or striker designed for this purpose only. Never light your torch with a cigarette lighter. Always light the fuel source first, then slowly crack open the oxygen valve to adjust to the desired flame type. Most soldering processes use a bushy blue flame.

(Continued on page 48)

Soldering CONTINUED

SOLDERING INSTRUCTIONS

1. Cut small squares of solder from the sheet. Be sure to clean your solder before cutting it. Separate these into small piles or store them in bags appropriately labeled.

2. Paint your joint, surrounding area, and solder with flux.

3. Using a bushy blue flame, slowly warm your chips of solder until they are suspended in a honey-like pool of flux. This consistency is ideal for transferring your solder to the joint. Place your balled up chips of solder directly on the joint with your pick.

4. Note the balled-up pallions of solder on the joint. (The flame has been removed to illustrate the detail.) Further heating at this point will allow the solder to flow.

STAGES OF FLUX

When heated, flux goes through a few stages. In the first stage, the flux turns chalky white and crusty as the water vapor leaves the flux. It is at this stage that chip solder placed on the joint can jump, which is why most jewelers use the transfer method and use a soldering pick.

In the second stage, the flux begins to bubble, which alerts you to the rising temperature.

In the third stage, the flux turns clear and fluid-like. It is at this stage that your temperature is high enough to make your solder flow. Further heating will produce unwanted results and eventually melt your work.

There is a small window of time before and after your work has reached the proper soldering temperature when you must work quickly. A few seconds is all the time you have to make sure your solder has flowed in all the right places. Continued heating at this stage will melt your work.

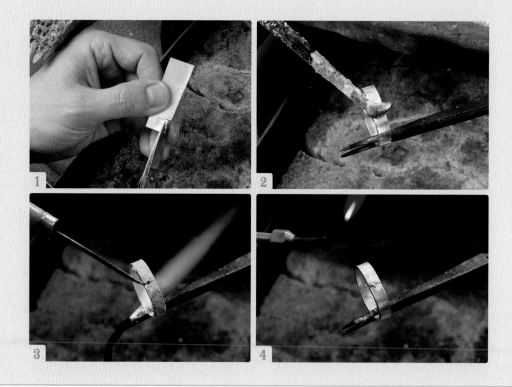

Water begins to evaporate

Bubbling begins

Reducing to fluid

Honey-like consistency

Clear fluid begins

Solder will flow

After soldering, let your work cool for a second, then use your copper tongs to place your work in the pickle pot for about five minutes. Remove, rinse, and dry your piece and wash your hands.

This soldering technique is nearly the same for gold. The difference is based on the gold karat you're attempting to solder. Each gold karat (14k, 18k, or 22k, for instance) has its own easy, medium, and hard solders, so choose one that matches the quality of gold.

FIRESCALE

Firescale happens during any torch-heating process, primarily during soldering. Oxidization of the copper content in the sterling occurs and is presented as a cloudy, bluish purple haze on the surface of your piece. Firescale is a common problem with sterling and can be quite frustrating. Firescale happens when your work is heated with a torch. Preventative products are available to combat firescale, but once it occurs only harsh sanding can remove it.

BASIC TECHNIQUE:

Drilling

Drilling is one of the first techniques jewelers should master. As straightforward as it sounds, there is still a series of instructions to follow.

A standard trigger-style drill has too much torque and speed for working with small-scale work and soft metals. Flexible-shaft and rotary tools make ideal jewelry-making drills; they are small and easy to handle. They typically come with an assortment of bits styles suitable for most projects. Look for drill models that come with a foot pedal or other speed-regulating device for added control. Some jeweler's drills feature a motor that is suspended above the workbench for easier handwork.

Most jewelers use tempered steel and twist-style drill bits, which are considered the universal drill bit for working with gold and silver. Specialty bits are customized for specific materials, such as glass, ceramic, plastics, even pearls, so they perform better than standard twist-style bits.

Typically, the smallest drill bit available at the hardware store is 1/16 inch (1.6 mm), and most jewelry work requires bits much smaller than that. Most jewelers use sizes #52 (0.0635 inch [1.6 mm]), #56 (0.0465 inch [1.9 mm]), #60 (0.04 inch [1 mm]), #68 (0.031 inch [0.79 mm]), and #70 (0.028 inch [0.71 mm]). These bits are sold individually through most jewelry suppliers or can be purchased as a set. Investing in a full jeweler's drill bit set is a good idea. Not only does a set allow for easy organization, it offers a wide range of drilling options for future projects.

Drilling is a one-way, one-chance technique. A drilled hole can always be larger, but it can never be made smaller. First drill a hole with a bit that is slightly smaller than necessary. Drill a hole a second time with a slightly larger bit, repeating the process and increasing the bit size as necessary until the desired diameter is reached. (Also, be sure to thread the object to be inserted through the hole every so often; it is surprising how quickly and subtly a hole can become too large.)

Drill bits come in a variety of sizes, and they are constructed from material as diverse as tungsten carbide, titanium nitride, and diamond coating. (A and B) sets of grinding burs in wooden boxes; (C and D) high-speed twist-style drill bits separated by size for easy reference; (E) assorted diamond-coated bits; (F) glass drill bits

DRILLING SAFETY CONSIDERATIONS

As with all techniques, always wear safety glasses when drilling, especially when using a flexible-shaft tool. High-speed twist drill bits break easily. It is important to drill slowly and apply even pressure. The life of your bits will be drastically extended if they are not overheated. If a bit is overheated just once, it is rendered useless. There are products available that can lubricate and cool the cutting blade during drilling, but dipping the bit in beeswax before starting will do the trick. When drilling, always sit upright and drill straight into your work. Angled holes increase the likelihood of breaking drill bits.

Determining the correct bit size depends on the task at hand. If you are drilling a hole for a rivet or pin, the diameter of the wire or tubing that will be threaded through the hole determines the size of the bit. Measure the rivet, pin, or threading material against the size of a bit using a caliper gauge. If you are drilling a hole for piercing, select the smallest bit that the saw blade will fit through.

DRILLING INSTRUCTIONS

1. Insert a drill bit that is *one size smaller* than the bit desired for the project into the drill and tighten it using the chuck key. Make sure to evenly tighten all three sides of the chuck.

2. Mark the drill holes with a center punch. Firmly secure your work with clamps or a vise. Drill the first hole slowly, and drill straight down into the work. Change to larger bits until the desired diameter is reached.

3. Long, unbroken curls of metal will be removed from the hole while drilling. If metal is flaking and shooting from the tip of the bit, the drill speed is too high. Ideally, a proper drill hole will yield two single, consecutive coils of metal.

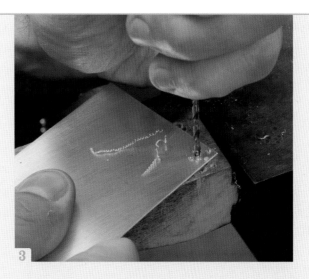

FINISHING TIPS

Removing broken drill bits. When drill bits break while drilling into metal, they frequently (and frustratingly) become lodged in the work piece. Steel drill bits are easily removed by submerging the work in an alum solution. The alum completely dissolves the broken bit, leaving the work piece intact. (Alum does not affect nonferrous metals.) Alum can be purchased at your grocery store in the spices section.

Removing the metal burr around the drill hole. Drilling leaves a rough burr on the outside lip of the hole. The burr can be removed with a bit that is three to four times the size of the hole. Holding the bit in your hand, gently twist it along the rim of the hole. The sharp, spiral edges will carve a shiny, beveled edge into the metal. Continue "shaving" the burr until the excess metal has been removed.

BASIC TECHNIQUE:

Sawing

A jeweler's saw is one of the top five basic jeweler's tools. Nearly every piece of jewelry requires the use of a jeweler's saw at some point.

Jeweler's saws can cut through just about anything, including fingers, so use caution. The jeweler's saw frame comes in a few different styles and qualities, most all of which have an adjustable model. They have thumbscrews for tightening the blade as well as adjusting the length. You don't need the most expensive, but be sure to buy one that adjusts.

Saw blades, sold by the dozen, range in size from 8/0 down to 0 then back up to 14. The finer, thinner blades are the 8/0 to 1/0, 8/0 being the thinnest and most fragile, and 1/0 being more durable for general cutting applications. A good starting size is a 2/0, which cuts most sheet metals without grabbing and is durable. If you buy a 0, 1, 2, 3, or higher they will have larger teeth and a coarser cut.

Photo: Grace Chin

SAWING INSTRUCTIONS

1. Choose a saw blade. Approximately seven to eight dozen thin blades are shown here.

2. Determine the direction of the teeth. Do this by running your finger down the length of the blade.

3. Begin loading your blade with the top thumbscrew first. The blade's tooth direction should face the handle. Place the blade in the top clamp and tighten the thumbscrew.

4. Place the other end of the blade in the bottom clamp.

5. Before tightening the clamp, apply pressure on the frame to create tension on the blade once tightened with the thumbscrew. You do not need a lot of tension; for a 2/0 blade about a ¼ inch (6 mm) of spring in the frame works.

6. To check for correct tension, thrum or pluck the blade. You should hear a high pitched noise that resonates. If you hear a dull thud, increase the tension.

7. Swipe your blade on a block of beeswax to help lubricate and cool the blade while you cut.

8. Cutting is almost always done at a rigid 45-degree angle to your work. Sit upright and let the tool do the work, as excess pressure will break the blades. Use the full length of your blade in long, continuous strokes. Sawing should be a smooth up-and-down motion.

Artist: Grace Chin
Title: *Bird in Paradise Necklace*
Materials: sterling silver, 10-karat gold
Techniques: Pierced, soldered

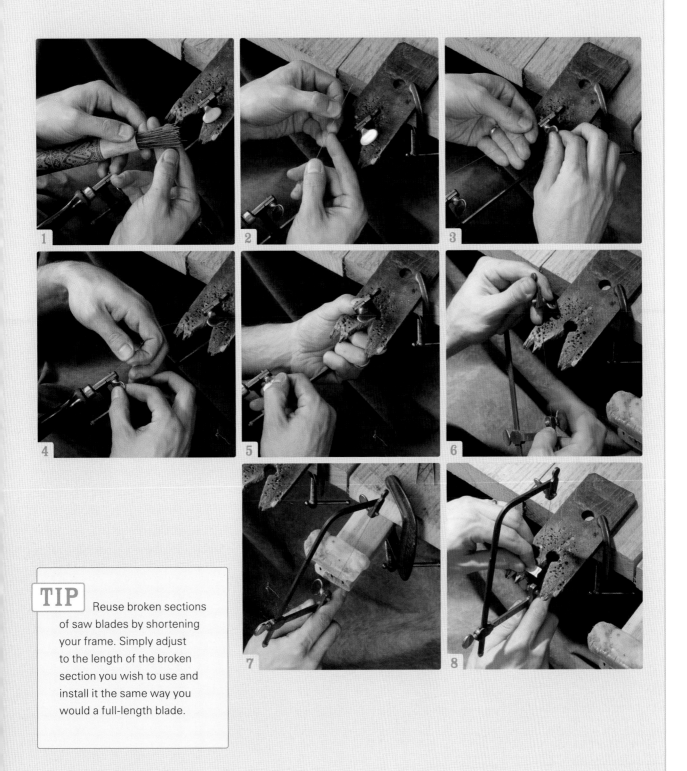

BASIC TECHNIQUE:

Filing

Filing is a necessary evil. It is essential for removing burrs, imperfections, ridges, ripples, and firescale in preparation for finishing processes such as sanding and polishing.

Simply push the tool across the metals surface with mild pressure and let the tool do the work for you. The most important thing to remember about filing is to never drag the tool back across the surface; it will dull your tool after time.

Files can take off large amounts of metal with just one swipe, so be sure to be conservative and gentle when working with delicate pieces. Files come in different sizes intended for different situations. Half round files are used for the inside of ring blanks.

Round files are used for cleaning tight curves and creating convex shapes. They can be used to cut shapes into metal for decoration.

To file inside pierced, flat work, first determine the shape that best suits your need. Flat files make your metal flat, square files make crisp 45-degree angles, triangular files make V shapes, round files make U shapes, and half round files make depressions. Try to imagine the opposing shape that will be created with your file. Play with your files on scrap metal.

FILING INSTRUCTIONS

1. To create flush, flat sides or crisp corners use flat files. Always support your work against your bench pin when filing. You can also use a ring clamp to hold just about any object. Move your file across the entire surface with one swipe. This will keep the work from becoming distorted or misshapen by working only one side at a time.

2. Half-round files, like the one shown here, are used for filing the inside of rings. They are usually tapered to accommodate various ring sizes. Be sure to make clean, even passes. If you angle the file slightly, you will begin to round or soften the ring shank. This rounding can be advantageous if making a comfort-fit shank.

3. Triangle-, square-, and round-needle files all can be used to carve designs. The ring shown is being decorated with a triangle-shaped file. The V-style impressions left from the file are used to add an intentional design around the entire band.

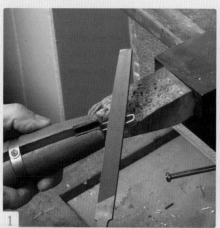

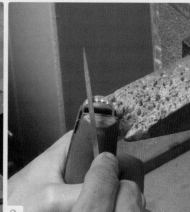

FORGING, FORMING, AND RAISING

All three of these terms involve the use of force to move metal.

Forming is the act of changing your metal's shape without displacing its mass or surface area. Simple bending is considered forming, as is taking a strip of sheet metal and bending it around a mandrel. You've changed the metal's shape without increasing the surface area. The same is true with folds, flaps, and bends, all of which change the metal's dimensions geometrically without changing its surface area.

Die-forming uses a bench press and a semi-rigid form to achieve the same results, although the surface area will sometimes increase. Die-forming uses a press to displace the metal around a shape. This technique can produce multiple, precise three-dimensional forms.

Forging is the act of using a tool (usually a hammer) to stretch, manipulate, and distort the metal from its original shape. The act is significantly different from simple forming because you are increasing the surface area of the metal. Depending on the shape of the tool, the metal will take on different directions. This is a controlled action.

Raising, a term used by silversmiths, is a form of forging, but with the element of dimension added. It is the act of taking a flat sheet of metal and "raising" it into a three-dimensional form such as a bowl. Using hammers to slowly and repetitively stretch and displace the metal around a domed or semirounded shape is considered raising. The principles behind raising are the same as forming.

All three of these techniques require constant annealing. Forging and raising require more annealing than forming due to the thinning of the metal. The thinning of the metal jeopardizes the metal's integrity and risks cracking.

CHASING

A form of forging, chasing is discernible by the use of steel tools bearing different imprints. Chasing tools are used in conjunction with a chasing hammer to add detail, subtle texture, words, or designs to the

Photo: Victoria Lansford

Artist: Victoria Lansford
Title: *Inspiraled*
Materials: sterling silver
Techniques: Repousse

metal surface. Chasing a finished piece of jewelry adds a distinct element of style that sets it apart from the crowd.

Making chasing tools can be rewarding. You can design a trademark pattern, imprint, or stamp that represents your work. Chasing tools can be easily made from sections of either round or square-shank tool steel. You can buy new tool steel from a supplier and order it to your desired lengths. This is ideal because tool steel comes annealed.

To make your own chasing tools, gather sections of annealed tool steel. Carving can be performed with files, burrs, and cut-off wheels used in your flexible-shaft tool. The important factor in making chasing tools is what you must do to the tool once you are finished with your design and before you begin using it. This process is called hardening and tempering, which makes the softer steel into tool steel. Tool steel, once tempered, can be used with hammers.

The process is simple. Once the design is complete, sand and polish the tip using your sanding sticks and buffer. Next, heat the tip of the tool with your torch until it appears reddish orange. Quench the tool in cool water immediately. At this stage the metal is hardened, but brittle.

The last step is to temper the steel. To temper, reheat the tip until a blue and yellow color appears. Quench the tool in cool water (remember to repeat these steps for the other end of the chasing tool where it will be struck repeatedly with a hammer). Once tempered, the tool is ready for use.

BASIC TECHNIQUE:
Finishing

Finishing uses simple tools, including sandpaper, a buffing machine, and the sanding and polishing sticks provided. Never skip a step in the finishing process. If you perform each step in its entirety, a mirrorlike finish can be attained. Finishing takes patience, and it is that patience that shows on a great piece of jewelry.

Making Your Own Sanding Sticks

To make your own sanding sticks, you will need a wooden yardstick, sheets of different grades of sandpaper, a scoring tool, and some rubber bands.

MATERIALS

- Wooden yardstick, cut into three 12" (30.5 cm) pieces
- Three sheets of sandpaper, one of each grit
- Sharp pointed tool, such as a scribe
- Small rubber bands

1. Place a sheet of sandpaper on a flat surface and align a piece of yardstick along the edge. Lightly score the paper, without cutting it, using a sharp pointed tool along the length of the yardstick edge.

2. Fold the stick on its edge. Score the next line the same as the first. The next score will be close to the original line. Be sure to score every corner fold; do not simply wrap the sandpaper around the stick.

3. Again score and fold. The most useful parts of this tool are the corners, which are used to sand crisp edges and make flush surfaces. Continue scoring and folding until the end of the sandpaper is reached. You should have a few layers of sandpaper tightly folded over the stick.

4. Wrap a rubber band around each end of the sandpaper to hold it in place. Small hair rubber bands seem to work best. Other holding devices such as staples will scratch your work if they accidentally make contact.

5. Repeat steps 1–4 to complete a stick for each grit.

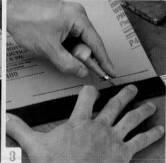
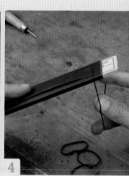

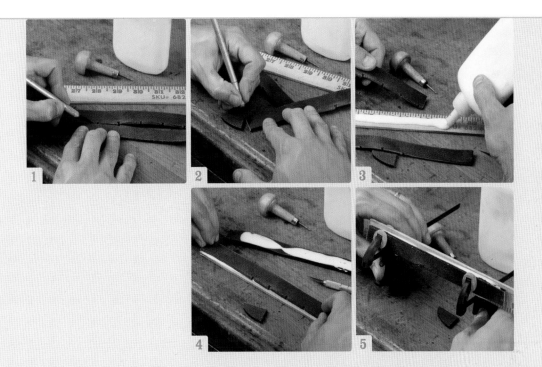

Making Your Own Polishing Stick

MATERIALS

- Wooden yardstick, cut into three 12" (30.5 cm) pieces
- Scraps of leather or suede, such as a worn-out belt
- Wood glue
- Clamps
- Cutting tool

A polishing stick is handy if you don't want to use a rotary-style buffing machine or if you're working with delicate or odd-shaped items. It has two sides—one for a fast-cut compound and one for a fine rouge that makes a great shine.

To make your own polishing sticks, you will need a wooden yardstick, strips of leather or felt, heavy-duty glue, and a razor blade.

1. Cut the leather into strips about the same size or smaller than your yardstick piece. For a wide leather belt as shown, a cut was made down the center.

2. Trim your leather to create two equal size pieces.

3. Apply a generous strip of glue to one side of the stick. Place the leather. Starting at the end, push out any air bubbles or ridges.

4. Apply glue to the other piece of leather and repeat step 3 on the other side of the stick.

5. Clamp the layer using small clamps and let dry overnight. Once the clamps are removed, apply a coat of rouge compound to one side and a bobbing compound to the other. Use like you would a sanding stick for a bright polish.

(Continued on page 58)

Finishing CONTINUED

1. Finishing begins with filing. See tips and steps in the Filing Basic Technique, page 54.

2. Sanding is the most important step in finishing. If you do not take care to sand correctly and completely, the polishing will show it. Sanding begins with a course-grit emery paper, usually around 220-, 320- or 400-grit depending on the severity of your file marks. Once the file marks have been completely removed, remove the delicate scratches left by the sandpaper. This is accomplished by using 600-, 800- or 1000-grit paper and completely removing the deeper scratches left by the previous papers. Always start with the coarsest papers and move incrementally up the highest grit available before attempting to polish.

3. Polishing should only be attempted once a superior finish has been achieved by sanding. It can be done using muslin or felt wheels attached to a mandrel inserted in your flexible-shaft tool. It is recommended to have three different buffs for each of the compounds.

| TIP | **Sanding Tips**

Be sure not to move backward in progress, say, by having sanded your work to a 1000-grit satin finish using emery paper then switch to a heavy-cutting compound on the buff. For instance, Tripoli is usually 600 grit. In this situation, skip to a higher grit compound such as rouge.

Start polishing with an abrasive compound such as Tripoli.

Next, move to a bobbing compound, a medium-cut compound, finally, finish your piece to a superior shine using very fine rouge. This final polish will create a mirror finish, highly reflective and beautiful. Be sure not to overload your wheels with too much compound. If you notice a cloudy surface, chances are you may have used too much compound.

BUFFING MACHINE TIPS

The same compounds and techniques are used with a miniature wheel in your flexible-shaft tool as they are with a full-sized buffing machine. When using a buffing/polishing machine, adhere to these general safety tips:

- Always wear safety glasses when polishing.

- Always firmly grip your piece using as many fingers as possible. Your work is frequently and quickly grabbed by the wheel and flung into the hood or across the room. A ring clamp makes an excellent holding device for polishing.

- Never polish chain using full size wheels. Even with the use of specific tools for polishing chain, it is still extremely dangerous. The wheel can grab and break the chain, and the possibility of entanglement with fingers is very real. Always polish chain using miniature wheels at slow speeds.

- Always dedicate each buff wheel to a specific material and compound. For instance, keep a set of buffs for polishing your steel tools. Small bits of steel left in the buffs can ruin softer metals pieces such as gold and silver. Keep a separate set of buffs (Tripoli, bobbing, and rouge) for gold and another set for sterling.

- Always polish on the bottom side of the wheel (not underneath, but slightly below the middle). This is the point where a small amount of pressure can be placed upward and away from you on the wheel.

Working with Other Materials

Jewelers have the ability to incorporate many different materials into their work. This is true with today's contemporary studio jewelers. The use of unconventional materials such as plastics alongside or in the absence of metal has become mainstream. Materials once viewed as eccentric have now been widely accepted by the industry. Examples include resins, paper, rubber, glass, even concrete. Not only do new materials share the space that was once reserved for precious and semiprecious stones, but they can be used in inventive ways that make the wearer feel just as luxurious. The following will cover some more popular materials, their uses, properties, and tolerances.

Artist: Brandon Holschuh
Title: *River Rock Ring*
Materials: Red rock, sterling
Techniques: Soldered, bezel set, distressed

A variety of precious and semiprecious stones: (A) Slab cut of rough material, parrot wing; (B) Slab cut of rough material, chrysoprase; (C) rough cut turquoise cabochon; (D) oval cabochon to be cut from agate outline; (E) selection of polished agate and quartz cabochon stones; (F) selection of faceted stones including orange citrine; (G) selection of faceted gemstones including diamond, opal, and ruby

PRECIOUS STONES

Conventional materials associated with making jewelry include faceted precious gemstones. Most minerals used for faceting are graded on hardness scale using the Mohs scale. Each precious mineral is tested for hardness against a softer mineral that can be scratched by it. This is important to bench jewelers and fine jewelers because they work with pricey gemstones and elaborate settings. When working with precious gemstones it is important to know, for instance, how hard emerald is compared to diamond. Likewise, how much heat can an emerald take? (Diamonds, for instance, can be cast directly in molten metal, but emerald cannot.) If you need to repair a setting containing a precious gemstone, questions like these will need to be addressed.

Faceted precious gemstones come in a variety of shapes and cuts, each presenting its own setting challenges to the jeweler. Shapes include round, square, oval, and rectangle, and they come in even more cuts, including fancy, princess, emerald, cushion, brilliant, and Asscher.

Moh's Scale

Hardness	Mineral
01	Talc
02	Gypsum
03	Calcite
04	Florite
05	Apatite
06	Orthoclase
07	Quartz
08	Topaz
09	Corundum
10	Diamond

Precious gemstone cutting, faceting, and polishing is an industry itself. The demand for beautiful, rare-cut gemstones has soared in recent years. (There are even entire television networks devoted to the sales of unmounted, loose gemstones.) Precious mineral deposits are being unearthed in remote reaches of the world every day. Explorations into the tundra or even under the sea bed are turning up huge caches of precious material suitable for the jewelry industry. New colors, new hybrids, and new compounds are introduced to the jewelry industry at a staggering pace. Keeping up with mineral origin, manufacture, and price is an ongoing preoccupation for most fine jewelers.

SEMIPRECIOUS STONES

Incorporating semiprecious stones in your designs is a great way to introduce bold, bright colors. Most nonfaceted gemstones and other minerals fall into the category of semiprecious stones, making them a significant part of the studio jeweler's repertoire. Beautiful, rich colors such as turquoises and coral are part of this family.

Lapidary work encompasses the act of cutting, grinding, faceting, and polishing precious and semiprecious stones. Stones can be cut, carved, and modified to fit into any design, although most jewelers start with the finished piece of semiprecious material and base their subsequent designs from the dimensions of the stone. Most semiprecious stones are polished; however, more and more are being faceted using the same techniques as precious stones. The standard shape for semiprecious stones is cabochon, which is a half dome shape with a flat back. This shape is easy to bezel-set and displays beautifully in most designs.

Some studio jewelers enjoy cutting their own stones. These lapidary working jewelers are able to create their own designs, shapes, and sizes using their own materials. This creates exceptional jewelry because the sizes and shapes are not commercially produced. To cut, carve, and polish your own stones you need a few basic lapidary tools, most of which incorporate water into the process, making for a messy studio. If you plan to incorporate this practice into your studio, separate this area from your metalworking area to avoid rusting your equipment and tools.

ABOVE
Artist: Brandon Holschuh
Title: *Inverted*
Materials: Citrine, sterling, 14-karat gold
Techniques: Pressure set, riveted, fabricated, assembled, soldered, oxidized

RIGHT
Artist: Todd Pownell
Title: *Garden and Diamonds*
Materials: Sterling, diamonds, emeralds
Techniques: Soldered, fabricated, set

Photo: Dan Fox

Unconventional and nontraditional resources can include the use of materials such as fur, bone, wood, hair, stone, glass, and dirt. When used appropriately, they can give your work a distinct mark of originality.

TIP **The Semantics of "Found" Art**

Found-object art is significantly different than intentionally deciding to work with an unconventional material. Found-object jewelry is exactly that—working with found objects. One might incorporate the use of an heirloom, relic, antique, or artifact or any "object" remarkably different than a material.

NONCONVENTIONAL MATERIALS

Nonconventional materials can really be anything at all. Eccentric designers incorporate vast and diverse materials into their work every day.

Most of these materials are commonly referred to as found objects, but they represent much more than that. When used wisely, these diverse materials can add purpose, depth, meaning, color, and texture to the work. Most times, the intent to work with unusual material is specific. This blanket term of found objects is commonly confused when an artist decides to work with a material purposefully because of its properties rather than the fact that it was "found."

Here is a list of just a few materials some current designers have been using in their work.

Dirt ages the work, adding the impression of having been unearthed from an archaeological site.

Wood adds warmth, color, hue, and tone; softens the work.

Glue allows cold connections on delicate materials.

Feathers add whimsy, dimension, and flow and create slow, kinetic movement.

Rubber adds color, movement, and texture.

Plastic adds multitude of colors and shapes, and allows for finishing treatments.

Resin can suspend objects that aren't able to be connected by glues or conventional settings.

Epoxy allows strong connections without the use of a torch.

Concrete adds novel design elements and can suspend objects; it can be used instead of conventional setting techniques.

Iron incorporates a natural mineral element texture and color when/if it rusts.

Horn introduces color variations not available in bone; adds texture.

Bone which is easy to work with, can be dyed, carved, polished, inlaid, and scrimshawed.

Photo: Grace Chin

Artist: Grace Chin
Title: *After St. Francis*
Materials: Resin, sterling, paper
Techniques: Fabricated, soldered

Porcelain can be heated and can be worked similar to glass.

Lava can be soldered on directly and adds texture and deep black color.

Stone can be cut, carved, drilled, and set; it adds a multitude of colors and textures.

Fur adds organic, soft texture.

Fiber introduces of movement, dimension, and texture.

Shell can be worked similar to bone; it adds soft, pale colors.

Teeth introduce natural organic elements; they can be carved, dyed, and polished.

Antler is worked similar to bone and horn; it adds intrigue.

Bakelite adds vast color, preformed shapes, and sizes.

Beach Glass introduces color and texture.

Hair (animal or human), can be tufted and used to add dimension and texture.

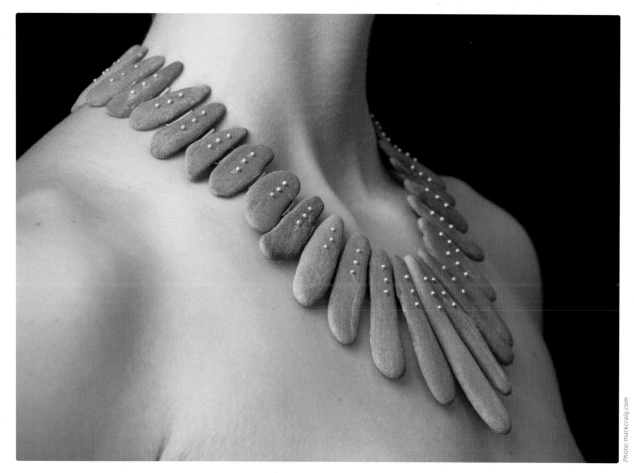

Artist: Andrea Williams
Title: *Sa Necklace*
Materials: sterling silver, beach stones
Techniques: Drilled, hinged, soldered, forged, polished

Properties of Stones and Unusual Materials

To work with unusual materials, you must first decide how you will incorporate them into your design. This planning is important because of the variations of material properties. For instance, if you decide to work with paper as your medium and you intend to incorporate it into your metal jewelry, you must do so after completion of the soldering and finishing techniques.

Most unconventional materials are *unconventional* because they pose a certain degree of difficulty working with them. They each must be analyzed and determined for durability, flammability, and whether they can be affixed. In most cases, materials cannot tolerate the heat from a torch, so soldering in and around the material is out of the question. Joints need to be done with cold connections, which are discussed in chapter 4 (see page 70). The use of glues, epoxy, and resin-type material can allow the maker to incorporate unconventional materials in their work.

When working with unusual materials, some overall caution needs to be taken. First, identify any material known to be toxic or hazardous. For instance, resins and plastics should never be cut, ground, or sanded without respiratory protection.

Drilling and Grinding Glass

YOU WILL NEED:

- Glass object to be worked, such as window pane glass, beach glass, or a glass lens
- Diamond-coated drill bit set and flexible-shaft tool
- Shallow pan or bowl filled with cool water
- Safety glasses

TECHNIQUE:

Simply handling glass poses a significant risk of injury. Glass is unpredictable and can crack and chip at any time. Protect your eyes by always wearing safety glasses.

First, soften the edges of any sharp areas of the piece. Flexible-shaft tools are ideal for use near water. The hazards are minimized due to the fact that the electrical motor portion is nearly 2 feet (61 cm) away. Do not use hand grinders that do not have a long flexible shaft; grinders that incorporate the motor into the hand piece pose a risk of electrocution when working with water. Grinding can also be performed partially submerged in water or just above the surface of the water. Frequently dip the object in the water to cool, irrigate, and remove debris from the work area.

Drilling glass underwater is different than normal drilling. First, a different kind of bit is used. Flat-headed, cylinder-style bits that are covered in a diamond abrasive coating slowly grind away fine bits of glass. It is during this process that the shape of the bit is removed from the material. Very light pressure should be applied when drilling into glass. Only enough pressure to create friction should be used. Be sure to have scrap wood or plastic behind the work to drill into. Always drill slowly and with even pressure and do not "push through" the piece. Reduce your pressure to very light when nearing the exiting of the bit from the other side; otherwise, you will get a large chip on the back side.

This technique can be applied to other materials such as stone and porcelain. Any material not affected by water may be drilled using water to minimize deterioration of the substance due to heat. The reason normal drill bits do not work with stone is because they heat up very quickly and become dull rendering them useless almost immediately.

Drilling and grinding in glass is best performed underwater. Because glass can chip, crack, and injure easily, you should wear eye protection. The water cools and lubricates the tool and material and also irrigates and rinses the debris from the work area.

DRILLING, GRINDING, AND WORKING PROPERTIES OF OTHER MATERIALS

When working with soft material such as bone, wood, and some plastics, remember not to use a lot of pressure or speed—both of which create heat and, in some cases, fire. Bone can burn and create a foul odor that permeates the room and lasts for hours. If you encounter any smell working with bone-like material you can be certain your speed or pressure is too high. Use manual files, sanding sticks, and hand drills to avoid any unwanted odor.

Toxicity is a significant health risk when working with unconventional materials. Fumes, particles, and debris can enter your body a variety of ways. Whether it be hand-to-mouth contact, inhalation, or simple cuts, hazardous material can wreak havoc on your body. The most common risk is particle inhalation. Dangerous particles enter the air when grinding on rusty parts, hard plastics, and resins. Always wear respiratory protection when drilling, grinding, or sanding dangerous materials. Be aware of the dangers when deciding to work with each material.

Photo: Doug Yaple

TOP
Artist: Dan Cook
Title: *Magnetically Held Bracelet*
Materials: Sterling, babinga wood,
neodymium magnets
Techniques: Riveted, assembled

OPPOSITE
Artist: Sarah Hood
Title: *Sanibel Island Rings*
Materials: Found organic materials
Techniques: Soldered, fabricated

Mechanics, Contraptions, and
Surface Treatments

One of the greatest joys for a jeweler is finding a clever solution to a design problem; this can also be one of the most frustrating challenges. All jewelers are faced with the same set of problems: determining size, streamlining function, or simply attaching a piece to the body. When these problems are solved imaginatively with resourcefulness such as smart mechanics and smooth functions, beautiful jewelry is created. Also, original, inventive, and artistic work gets noticed. This chapter teaches jewelry mechanics, contraptions (including findings and cold connections), and surface treatments (including polishing and distressing).

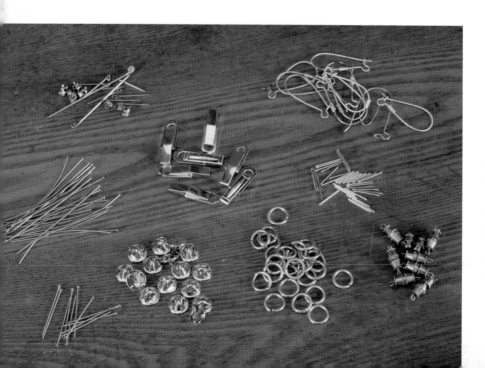

LEFT Examples of store-bought findings, jump rings, clasps and earring wires. Many of these findings can be made by hand and integrated into your designs.

OPPOSITE
Artist: Brandon Holschuh
Title: *Caged*
Materials: Sterling, turquoise
Techniques: Soldered, fabricated, flame beading, fused

Cold Connections

Cold connections are defined as any connection that does not require the use of torch heat or solder to join separate pieces of material. They can be made in a variety of ways to achieve the same result.

RIVETS

Made with solid wire or hollow tubing stock, rivets are used frequently in jewelry applications and are the primary source of cold connections. They can be long, short, wide, or thin, and can be used to bond just about any material. Rivets can be hidden, showcased, and even made to disappear.

Rivets are attached with pressure when finishing or completing the joint. This is usually done with a flaring tool or a riveting hammer.

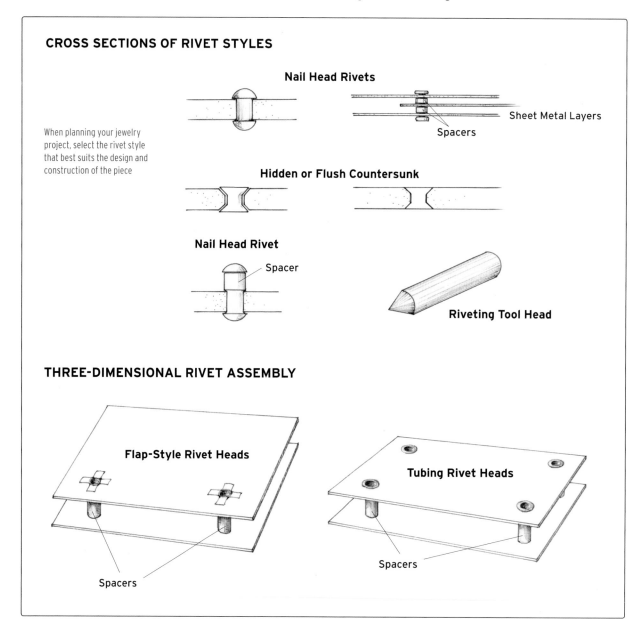

CROSS SECTIONS OF RIVET STYLES

When planning your jewelry project, select the rivet style that best suits the design and construction of the piece

Nail Head Rivets

Sheet Metal Layers

Spacers

Hidden or Flush Countersunk

Nail Head Rivet

Spacer

Riveting Tool Head

THREE-DIMENSIONAL RIVET ASSEMBLY

Flap-Style Rivet Heads

Tubing Rivet Heads

Spacers

Spacers

Wire Rivet

Wire rivets are made from solid wire. Use the thickest wire possible (14, 16, or 18 gauge) for the application. Wire higher than 20 gauge should be reserved for intricate, delicate work.

To make a wire rivet, measure the thickness of the layers of material you intend to join. This could be any material sandwiched by two outer sheets of metal or any material alone. Rivets can be added in any material that is able to be drilled and hard enough to endure mild pressure.

Once the thickness of the metal is measured, add a few millimeters on either side to the total length of wire needed to form the rivet heads. Then, drill the material or metal with an appropriate size drill bit. Keep a chart near your workbench of the comparison between wire diameter to drill bit size (below).

Wire Gauge to Corresponding Drill Bit Sizes

Gauge Wire	Drill Bit Size
6	20
8	30
10	38
12	45
14	51
16	54

Next, insert the section of wire through the drilled hole. Place the piece on a steel bench block or anvil face. Using a riveting hammer, gently tap the end of the wire to flatten. Immediately turn the piece over and gently tap the other side of the wire face the same way. Continue flipping the piece over and with gentle pressure create tiny mushroom heads on either side. While forming the heads on the ends of the wire, gently make circular motions with your hammer while tapping to round the head while flattening. It's important that both sides have equal parts wire.

TIP   Cool Tool

A great tool for cutting equal lengths of wire and tubing for making rivets is a tube cutting jig. This tool is used to hold tubing and wire at specified lengths for cutting. It has a slot for your jeweler's saw and an adjustable screw to set the length.

Tubing Rivet

Creating a rivet out of tubing uses the same principle as wire rivets but uses a different pressure method. With tubing, you still need to measure the thickness of your materials, add a few millimeters and drill out your hole that corresponds with the outside diameter of the tubing. Instead of creating a mushroom-style head as with wire, use a riveting tool to flare the tubing outward while flattening it onto the surface of the material. A riveting tool is usually made from a center punch but can be any shaft-style tool that has a soft but steep point that can be used to flare the end of the tubing. Polish the steel tool to avoid marring the metal.

Once the tubing has been flared, flip the work over and do the same, checking for alignment so that both ends have the same amount of material. Continue this process until the metal cannot be flared using the tool alone. At this point, set the work piece on a steel bench block or anvil face and use your riveting hammer to gently tap all around the face of the rivet to create a wide, donut-shaped head. Continue to flip the work over to avoid distorting the other side. The trick is equal tapping and lots of practice.

How to Make a Tubing Rivet

YOU WILL NEED:

- Jeweler's Saw
- Tubing
- Strips of sheet metal
- Riveting hammer
- Flaring tool
- Flexible shaft tool and drill bit set

BELOW LEFT This basic cold connection rivet requires no soldering

BELOW RIGHT A flaring tool can be any dull pointed tool that shapes the tubing outward. The tool pictured is a slightly polished center punch; notice the angled tip.

TECHNIQUE:

1. Drill holes in both pieces of sheet metal with a bit that is the same size as your tubing. Slide the parts down and onto the tubing to test for fit. The fit should be snug but free moving.

2. Cut the tubing within a millimeter or two of either side of the joint. You need to have a good amount of tubing to create the rivet head. With a flaring tool and medium pressure, flare the tubing outward.

3. A spacer is a sleeve of oversized tubing that fits over the original tubing. The (copper) spacers inside the tubing diameter should measure the same as the original (sterling) tubing's outside diameter. They should fit snugly, nestled inside one another.

4. Tap all around the edge of your flared tubing with a riveting hammer. This gentle motion curls the metal and forms the round rivet head. Do not use excessive force; small taps work better than swift blows to create a uniform donut shape.

5. Movement is created by opposing motion of the strips of metal. If the rivet is too tight, there will be excessive friction, leading to stiff or lack of movement. The movement should be smooth and fluid.

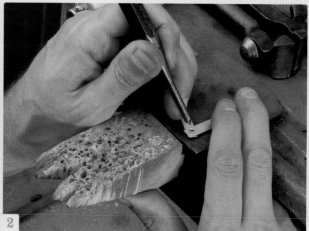

TOP For installing a spacer in your rivet, measure the clearance needed between the materials being riveted. The spacer should be cut to the same size.

MIDDLE When forming the rivet head, be sure to place the materials on a steel bench block and turn the piece over repeatedly, creating even rivet heads on both sides.

BOTTOM A simple cold connected rivet can also make a basic hinge: a small scrap of paper or cardboard inserted between the strips during the riveting process doubles as a washer. It can later be removed with water or flame, allowing just the right amount of movement.

Spacer

If the objects or materials to be riveted require a bit of clearance, you will need to make and install a spacer, which allows a rivet thicker than the materials to be riveted. This is handy for riveting multiple layers that may need to have spaces in between them.

To install a spacer, first decide the total length of the rivet needed, then decide how much space in between you need. Subtract the clearance needed from the total length to determine the size of your spacer. To cut a section of tubing to use a spacer, you will need tubing that will fit around the *outside* of your wire or tubing.

To determine the size of tubing needed for the spacer, use this tip: If you are using 18-gauge wire for your rivet, you should know that it is 1.02 mm thick, so in order to find tubing that your wire will fit through it should have an *inside* diameter of at least 1.02 mm. Depending on the manufacturer or if you are making the tubing yourself, test-fitting is the best recommendation. Once you have cut the section of tubing that will be used as a spacer, simply slide it on during your assembling process and rivet.

Flap-Style Rivet

A flap-style rivet, made from tubing, uses the same principle as the other rivets, but instead of a donut or mushroom shape on the head, flaps hold the materials in place.

Flaps can be used as decoration or just for more holding power if hammering is not an option. They are similar to metal fold-down tabs used on envelopes. Because they have to be cut down the shaft, flap-style rivets require more material than a standard rivet, so give yourself a little extra material to work with. Fold the flaps over using flat-nosed pliers, then use a riveting hammer to make them flush against the surface of your materials.

One-Sided Rivets

A one-sided rivet is used to install a part that you would like to affix from behind. One-sided rivets use wire or tubing that is soldered in place on the back side of the part. Once soldered, the part can be affixed to another flat piece of material via a one-sided rivet. The part acts as a head and the pressure is created from riveting the back side only. This is an excellent solution for mounting metal designs in material that cannot be soldered, such as wood.

Flush Rivets

Flush rivets, also known as hidden or disappearing rivets, contains holes that have been countersunk. This means that the material to be riveted is drilled as normal, but when finished a larger bit is inserted into the hole opening and a bevel (a countersinking) is cut out. The rivet is fed through the hole and riveted as normal, but during the process the metal expands into the countersunk area instead of building up on the surface. The head is then filed off and sanded flat. The pressure is held from under the surface. Flush rivets are used to disguise a needed rivet where one may not be aesthetically pleasing.

NAILS

Nails are created the same way as rivets. Using a heavy gauge such as 14 or 16, hold a section of wire in a clamp or hand vice, tap the end of the wire with a riveting hammer until a mushroom shape is made, then cut the nail to the desired length and sharpen the opposing end. Nails were once made by hand using this very technique. Early wooden structures such as barns and stables were made with hand-wrought nails. Nails for jewelry applications can be used if working with wood or for repairing old wooden jewelry tools such as hammer handles and boxes.

SCREWS

Screws can be made from sterling silver, gold, or any other nonferrous metal. A screw is a tapered, threaded, cylindrical pin with a head at one end that is fitted with a tool to twist it into a hole. Variations of screws can be used as a fastener or for applying force like in a clamp. Bolts are made the same way as screws. Nuts can be made as well to fit corresponding screws. All of these styles can be made with simple wire, tubing, and a miniature jeweler's tap and die set.

A simple threaded bolt can be a useful cold connection. When attempting to secure something that cannot be drilled or fitted with a rivet, you can make an armature of sorts and create tension from all directions with the use of threaded screws.

To make a screw or bolt, locate the correct die to begin cutting the thread onto the wire. Use a heavy-duty wire such as 14 or 16 gauge. Sterling silver screws made with 18-gauge wire and higher are delicate, so take caution when working with that gauge wire. Once you decide which size die the wire should be threaded into, begin by slightly sharpening the end of the wire. The sharpened end makes for easier initial entry into the cutting teeth of the die.

The inside of the die cuts tiny grooves around the outside wall of the wire as it is twisted into the hole. These grooves (threads) are cut deeper and deeper as they move up the length. Occasionally back the wire out of the die and clean the debris from the inside cutting teeth and along the threads. When threading the wire, do not force the wire through; let the tool do the work.

You can create a head on the other end of the threaded rod by heating it with a torch until it balls up. This process is the same as making a headpin. File the head of the ball flat to create a screwlike shape. You can even cut a slot in the face of the head for fitting with a tiny screwdriver. If you wish to make a corresponding threaded hole for your screw or its own nut, you will need to use a tap.

A tap looks similar to a screw but instead of threads it has cutting teeth that cut the corresponding grooves into the inside wall of the hole being fitted for a screw. To make a hole for a threaded screw, drill out the hole slightly smaller than the diameter of the wire used for the screw. Insert the corresponding tap in the hole and begin twisting with mild pressure (excessive pressure will strip the action). Once the grooves are

Artist: Brandon Holschuh
Title: *Not for Sale*
Materials: Amazonite,
sterling, copper
Techniques: Soldered, cold
connected, fabricated, drilled

Making Jump Rings

YOU WILL NEED:

- Round-nosed pliers
- Flat-nosed pliers
- 18- or 20-gauge wire
- Jeweler's saw
- Various sized straight mandrels (not tapered)
- Bench pin

TECHNIQUE:

To make jump rings from wire stock, first you must decide what sized jump rings you need to make. For instance, if you plan on suspending some tiny delicate pearls from an earring post, you would need a skinny mandrel and high-gauge thin wire.

To make jump rings, wrap the wire around the mandrel as many times as needed to make the desired number of jump rings (one wrap around the mandrel produces one jump ring). Once complete, slide the "spring" off the mandrel and hold it with your round-nosed pliers against your bench pin. Begin cutting each ring from the spring using your jeweler's saw. As each jump ring falls off you will notice a very slight kink to each one; once loaded in place, close the gap of the jump ring using flat-nosed pliers.

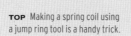 **Jump Ring Tip**

Use a disposable wooden mandrel such as a pencil, chopstick, or dowel. Once wrapped, keep the spring in place and cut through the wood and spring using your jeweler's saw. This technique allows you to hold the spring more firmly with the wood and does not allow much movement during cutting. The wooden dowel is destroyed for each batch of jump rings but many find it easier to work with.

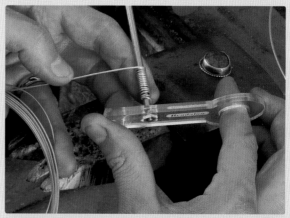

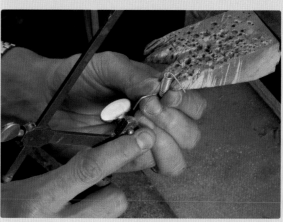

TOP Making a spring coil using a jump ring tool is a handy trick.

BOTTOM Always use a jeweler's saw to cut your jump rings. A jeweler's saw makes flush, flat cuts and produce tight fitting jump closed jump rings.

established, the teeth will continue to slowly remove material from the grooves. Occasionally back the tap out and clean the tool and hole of shavings.

Once complete, the tool should thread in and out of the hole with no friction. Remove the tool and insert the corresponding screw. Tap and die sets are measured in either metric or inches, although most jewelers use metric. Bolts for screws are made the same way, but are drilled into thicker heavy tubing, then filed flat on the sides in the shape of a bolt. Wing-style nuts can be made with flat sheet metal and a few twists.

JUMP RINGS

Jump rings are used frequently to make cold connections. Although they can be used without soldering to secure items if a torch is not available, they are strengthened by soldering. Jump rings, along with headpins, screws, and nails, can easily be made, although most of them are available from suppliers.

HEADPINS

A headpin is the universal term for a holding rod. You can make it with or without a torch. Most headpins are made, without a torch, using the nail-making technique, although a thinner wire should be used and the length extended. Headpins, similar to an axle or hinge pin, are normally used to secure a part or complete a hinge.

EARWIRES

Earwires are hook-style earring posts. They allow movement that post styles cannot. Ear wires can be made in many different styles, but most are made with 18-, 20-, or 22-gauge wire. Standard wire posts are made with 20-gauge wire. Anything thicker than 18 gauge becomes uncomfortable in the ear. Simple wire wrapping, bending, and curving styles are all cold-connected. Ear wires can be made by cutting two exactly same lengths of wire, bending the swoop shape with round-nosed pliers, and finishing them with a small ring shape. Be sure to sand and polish

any rough, sharp edges from the ends, as they can irritate the ear when inserted.

Settings

Settings attach, hold, or secure an object with metal. Settings can be very simple or very complex. Most setting styles address faceted precious or semiprecious stones.

BEZEL

Bezel is a basic but functional style of setting. It uses a continuous band of metal that wraps all the way around the circumference of the object to hold it in place. There are no prongs. Although the technique is relatively easy, it takes a special eye to decide if a bezel setting will work with a stone. Most cabochon-style stones can be bezel set. Stones or objects with flat backs and soft edges work best with a bezel setting.

PRONG

Prong settings can vary greatly but the principle is universal. The size of the stone usually determines the number of prongs. Large stones can be held with as little as four prongs, but they need to be thick, sturdy, and strong. Small stones can be held with as little as three prongs. Prongs can be made to fit a specific design or they can be commercially purchased for the correct size stone.

Simple soldering and wire will make basic basket-style prongs. To correctly set faceted stones using prongs, they need to be notched. Notching a prong takes skill, so don't get discouraged on your first try. Notching requires the use of stone-setting burrs and a flexible-shaft tool. It is best to attempt with bright light, a stable work bench, and magnification. Because the notches are so small on the inside of the prong, practice first on a scrap piece of wire. The notch must be cut into all the prongs at the same level or the stone will appear crooked. The notches cannot be too deep or the prong will collapse when you try to apply pressure with a tool.

BELOW
Artist: Todd Pownell
Title: *Snow Storm*
Materials: Gold, diamonds, sterling
Techniques: Soldered, fused, constructed

OPPOSITE
Artist: Brandon Holschuh
Title: *Hold on*
Materials: Oversized stone, prong set, sterling silver
Techniques: Hand-fabricated and soldered

Photo: Dan Fox

PRESSURE

Pressure setting is another master jeweler technique. Pressure-setting a stone requires lots of talent, skill, and mastering. When done correctly, this style of setting will appear to have a stone floating in between two pieces of metal. Most pressure setting is done with diamonds due to their relative strength; it is not advisable to pressure-set any object or stone that may be vulnerable to cracking or breaking. Pressure setting requires a spring-like action to force two opposing faces of metal at one another. After creating small grooves, the shape of the edges of the stone are cut into the faces of the opposing metal, and the stone clicks into place. Pressure setting requires thick, heavy metal to be used as the spring.

BEAD SET

A common setting style, bead setting has nothing to do with the kind of beads that require stringing. In bead setting, you create tiny balls of solid metal on the surface of the jewelry using bead-setting tools. These tiny beads, or bumps, of metal are made by pushing tiny curls of metal across the surface using a graver. These beads are formed by tiny inverted cups at the tip of the tool that create the bump or dome shape. The bead-setting tool set has many different size heads that create various size beads.

PAVE

Pave setting is nearly the same as bead setting, but in pave setting the tiny stones are pushed against one another so close that you cannot see much metal. This practice is referred to as pave because you essentially pave the surface of the jewelry with stones. This technique is reserved for the very patient, very meticulous, very careful master jeweler. (Some jewelers are strictly stone setters of expensive, rare stones.) When done correctly, pave setting is breathtaking.

CHANNEL

Channel setting is also found in jewelry applications. When setting a stone, a channel is cut into the inside face or wall of the metal using a stone-setting burr. The stone or series of stones are usually slid into place in the channel.

Contraptions

Contraptions, or mechanisms, can encase, enclose, hold, suspend, or attach, and can be elaborate, decorative, or hidden. In the commercial fine jewelry industry these are often called findings.

They can be made without the use of a torch but most require it. Contraptions are a fun problem-solving design element in jewelry making; let your imagination build on the following ideas.

CLASPS

A clasp is any device, usually of metal, made to fasten two or more of the same parts or ends. When executed well, they are seamless within the design of the jewelry. In most cases, clasps are required on bracelets and necklaces. Standard clasps such as lobster claw are commercially available and work great, but most studio jewelers enjoy the challenge of designing their own, incorporating their own style into their work. Clasps and closure devices are the most challenging mechanism in jewelry design.

CATCHES

Catches are similar to clasps but usually have a spring-loaded feature. Catches can be just as decorative and ornate as clasps, and they may actually have a second or third mechanism built into the design to ensure they do not come undone. Some standard styles are box catches and spring catches, which are used on hair barrettes or pin backs.

CAPS

Caps can be used to secure, but most are intended to dress up a bead or pearl. They are usually made by the jeweler, although many styles are commercially available. Simple caps can be made to custom-fit a specific sized bead. They are becoming more popular due to the trend in glass bead making. Quite a few glass artists enjoy making beads and like to incorporate simple metalworking into their designs.

BAILS

Bails are devices used to attach a pendant to a chain. The simple bail can be just a jump ring, but most are ornate and serve a purpose while adding to the design. A bail allows the pendant to swing from side to side and front to back. Bails can be made with or without solder, but most are made to match the design of the piece.

Artist: L. Sue Szabo
Title: *Roji Stones*
Material: sterling silver
Techniques: photo etched, fabricated, hinged, patinaed

How to Make a Bead Cap

YOU WILL NEED:

- Heavy hammer
- Disc-cutting tool
- Round-nosed pliers
- Flat-nosed pliers
- 24- or 26-gauge wire
- Jeweler's saw
- Various sized straight mandrels (not tapered)
- Bench pin

TECHNIQUE:

Decide how much of the end of your bead you would like covered. If you want more bead covered, choose a larger disc hole. Then insert 24- or 26-gauge sheet metal into the appropriate slot. Strike the punch with a fast and hard blow. The disc-cutting tool is designed to cut with one forceful strike, not many small strikes, with the heavy hammer. Once the discs are cut, clean up the sharp edges using a file or sanding stick. Begin doming with the largest dome and largest punch possible, then slowly work up to smaller ones while moving the work from dome to dome. Once the desired size is achieved, drill your hole using the smallest hole possible for your string; this secures the bead once strung with other beads.

TIP | Setting the Cap

To secure your caps to the bead itself, use a tubing rivet. Drill out the cap with a hole large enough to accept the tubing. Measure your tubing and inset with the caps through your bead. Cut, file, then flare your tubing using the same technique as riveting. Use a riveting hammer to complete the technique.

Enclosures

Enclosures are devices that house objects or materials, and are used frequently in jewelry though they may go unnoticed. They can be as simple as a cage or as complex as a box, cradling gemstones, framing found objects, and more.

CAGES

Cages hold objects that are misshapen, delicate, or cannot be attached by any other means. Cages are normally built from wire, but can be made from any material and interpreted many ways. It is the interpretation of this generalized holding device that is most fun. Cages can be round, square, rectangle, even flat, they can have doors that open, slide or hinge, and they can even have a floor or base. The cage should be constructed around the object, and just outside its dimensions. The object should be held by the cage, not be rattling around inside.

ARMATURES

Armatures, like cages, hold an object that can't be attached to your work by any other means. They are designed with your object or material in mind. Armatures can be made from simple wire-working skills or can incorporate complex soldering joints. They are used in museums for displaying artifacts. If you've ever wondered how that shard of Roman pottery is gracefully suspended, an armature was built with the shape of the object in mind.

FRAMES

Jewelry frames serve the same purpose as household frames. They can be made of any flat material, although most jewelry frames are made from metal. They are ideal for showcasing miniature pictures and or clippings. With the combined use of rivets and frame, you can create miniature memories in jewelry. Frames are easy to cut out using your jeweler's saw and can be made to fit any size. A template is recommended to be sure sizing is equal around all of the sides. Frames can be used with a backing plate, joining and the two layers using rivets.

BOXES

Boxes house an object not meant to be seen. Boxes in jewelry applications have been around for centuries. Reliquaries were used in religious art from as early as the twelfth century to hold sacred saint relics, such as a bone. Boxes are a bit more challenging to make than most contraptions. You must be good at measuring, soldering and a few other techniques before attempting to make a box. Boxes can be sealed, open, or have a lid. Studio jewelers have made boxes for rings, necklaces, and earrings.

HINGES

Hinges are built to allow a pivoting action. They are not always associated with box lids or doors, though when used wisely, hinges can be an integral part of a design. For instance, to create unidirectional movement in a bracelet, you would need to incorporate hinges into the design. Hinges can be complex or simple. Most hinges are constructed with tubing and wire, similar to a rivet. The factor that allows movement is the joint between your work and the hinge. Hinges can be found on most belt buckles, pin stems of brooches, and of course boxes. They can be spring-loaded, hidden, and even the focus of the design.

LATCHES

Latches incorporate a hinge and an additional moving part to create a safety. Latches look, work, and act just like the larger versions but on a smaller scale. They can be used with frames, boxes, and lids. You can make an extra part for your latch if you want a hasp style.

Surface Treatments: Patinas, Textures, and Finishes

Any alteration, process, chemical, treatment, or tool affects the way metal looks. Even air and water affect metal by the natural process of tarnishing. Patina solutions, heat treatment, tooling, buffing—the possibilities are endless—are all ways to alter the look of metal whether you're after an aged finish or a shiny one.

PATINAS

Patina is a fine coating of oxide on the surface of metal. Usually synonymous with the blue-green color found on old copper or bronze objects, this natural aging process can sometimes be forced with patina solutions.

Recipes have been created over the years to patina all nonferrous and ferrous metals. The most common and quickest way is with chemical treatments, and the most popular chemical that works on most metals is hydrochloric acid. This acid is found in most mixtures available from metal suppliers to darken or color your metal green, blue, or black. Be sure to read all warning and use labels on any chemical.

The metal most susceptible to patina is copper. Copper can be manipulated to exhibit a rainbow of colors. Deep reds and oranges can be achieved simply by heating gently with your torch flame. Another simple recipe is to spray warmed copper with peanut oil.

A fun experiment is to mist your copper with a solution of water and sprinkle with salt. Vibrant blues and greens can be achieved by placing your work under a glass pie cover with a small cup of ammonia next to it. Sit back and watch the chemical reactions color the surface of your metal.

A word of caution when mixing and performing patina recipes: in most cases they are toxic. Even mixtures of household items can be harmful. Do your research. Many online sources have great recipes for antiquing, aging, and coloring your metals, but you must read all caution statements and heed their warnings.

Rust on steel is another example of, usually unwanted, patina. You can create rust in about twenty-four hours by scratching the metal with a scouring pad, misting with water, and letting it dry in the sun. If it's rust you *don't* want, be sure to keep your studio tools dry.

TEXTURE

Texture can be achieved by a variety of methods, including this list of common techniques:

Artist: Brandon Holschuh
Title: *Kinetic Bracelet*
Materials: Copper, brass, sterling
Techniques: Forged, soldered, riveted, flame beading, drilled, assembled

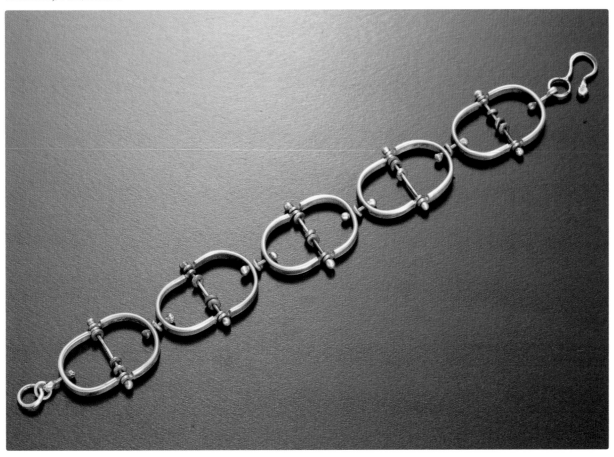

Finishing Attachments for Your Flexible Shaft Tool

TOP LEFT The **sanding disc** attachment creates distinct semicircle scratches. The angle the flexible-shaft tool is held and the speed with which the tool is used will alter the results.

BOTTOM LEFT The **hard rubber wheel** attachment makes small dimples or cups similar to a hammered finish. It actually pushes the metal around and can quickly distort your work. Use caution and work with a gentle hand when using this tool.

TOP RIGHT The **scouring pad** method produces a dull, matte finish by making tiny scratches all over the surface to reveal brightness but not a polish. This technique is great for removing scratches left by file marks and quickly removing lots of surface imperfections.

BOTTOM RIGHT The **soft rubber wheel** makes a shiny texture but not a polish. It works by heat caused by the friction of the spinning tool. This hot rubber beats the metal to a shine. You can burn the surface of the metal with this attachment, and your work quickly gets hot, so keep your fingers away.

ABOVE A **muslin buffing wheel** is used to put a high reflective polish on the surface of metal. Muslin buffs can be used with various polishing compounds to achieve polished results varying from high polish to mirror finish.

TOP LEFT **Wire wheels** come in steel and brass, each producing its own unique surface treatment. A wire wheel produces a shine but not a mirror finish. Wire wheel texture is a great all-around finish.

BOTTOM LEFT The "lap" style **split mandrel** attachment uses coiled strips of various grits of sandpaper. The strips are inserted into the slot on the shaft and wind around the mandrel. When using this tool a repetitive lapping of the sandpaper makes for a unique texture. This is a great tool for sanding the inside of ring shanks too.

Tooled

Tooled surface treatments are diverse. You can use steel tools to texture the surface of your metal with unique results. Play with different tools to texture a piece of scrap metal. Try dimples, ridges, cuts, gashes, and various other treatments to achieve your own results.

Burnished

A burnished surface is achieved using a highly polished steel tool. The softness of the polished steel creates a shiny scratch on your metal. This burnishing technique creates very reflective results without the use of polishing wheels and compounds. Various-shaped burnishing tools are available. The most common use of a burnishing tool is bezel setting. The burnishing tool puts a smooth, shiny finish around your bezel-set stone, making it an excellent finishing technique.

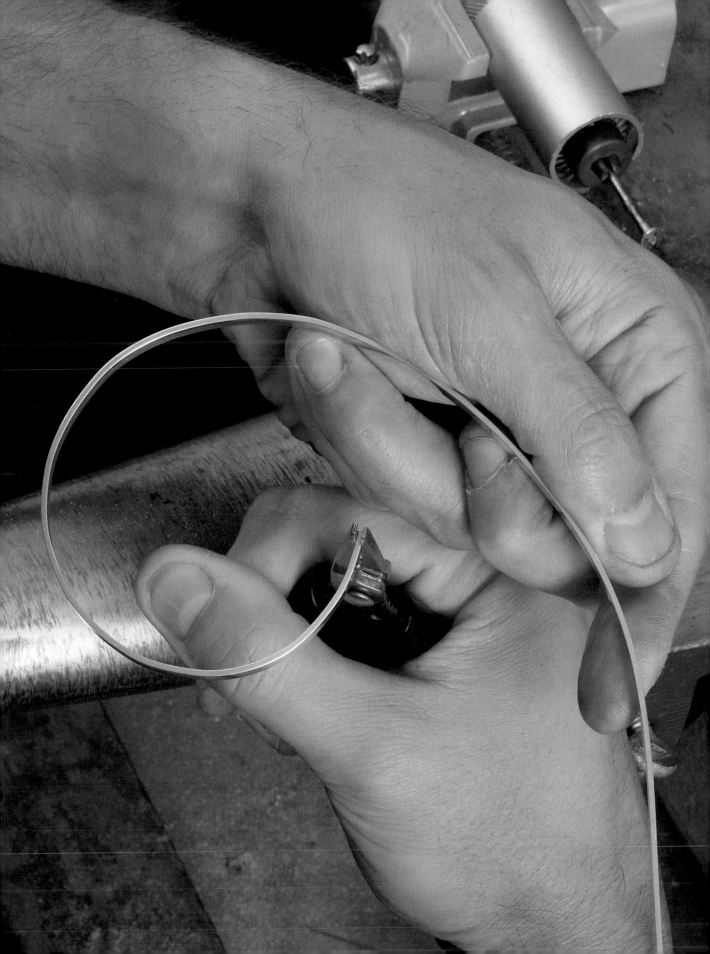

PART
2

In the Jeweler's Studio:
The Projects

Simple
PROJECT: Band Ring

The simple band ring is the simplest basic ring blank to make. This project is versatile, with its unlimited variations, and it is the foundation for other projects in this book. Once finished, the simple band ring can be textured, soldered again, and set with stones. In addition to honing basic metal-forming skills, this project teaches how to size rings with a mandrel.

TOOLS

- Ring mandrel
- Scribe
- Jeweler's saw
- Flat-nosed pliers
- File
- Third hand
- Soldering tweezers
- Flux
- Jeweler's snips
- Soldering torch set
- Slotted sandpaper mandrel bit
- Soldering pick
- Copper tongs
- Pickle solution
- Bench block or anvil
- Rawhide mallet
- Sanding stick
- Flexible-shaft tool
- Slotted sandpaper mandrel bit
- Scouring pad

MATERIALS

- 5 mm × 1.25 mm sterling silver sizing stock (wide, flat wire can also be used)
- Sterling silver sheet solder (hard)
- Black patina solution

INSTRUCTIONS

Shaping

1. Measure sizing stock to the desired ring size; for this project, size 8 has been chosen. On most ring mandrels, small numbers are located along the side for this purpose. Score your mark for the desired length with a scribe.

2. Using a jeweler's saw with a 2.0 blade, cut the sizing stock at your mark.

3. Using flat-nosed pliers, begin shaping the ring. Sizing stock of this gauge bends with medium force. For shaping, use only pliers with smooth jaws; pliers with teeth will mar the surface.

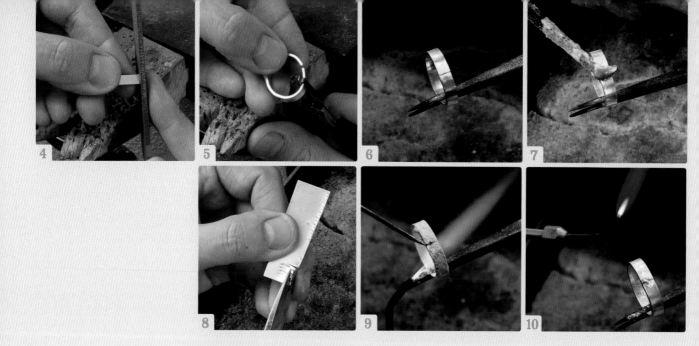

4. File the edges flush before closing the ring shape. The joint needs plumb square edges to fit together with no gap.

5. Begin to close the ring shape with pliers. Be sure to line up the edges flush against one another. The joint should be nearly seamless. This step is essential preparation for soldering. Solder will not fill gaps. It is not necessary to have a perfect round ring shape at this stage. Your ring should be egg shaped with the joint nearly flat.

Soldering

6. Prepare for soldering by mounting the ring on the third hand. Soldering tweezers are secured to a heavy base for this step.

7. Paint flux on and around the joint to be soldered.

8. Cut small squares of hard solder using the jeweler's snips. These are called chip solder pieces. You will need two or three small pieces for this project. Be sure to paint each of these with flux, too.

9. Using a bushy, blue flame, heat the chips of solder on the firebrick until they ball up. Pick up the balls of solder using your soldering pick. The warmed flux acts like honey, sticking to the pick, allowing the balls to be easily moved. Place the balls on the ring. Keep the piece warm with the flame while placing one or two balls of solder directly on the joint.

10. Once your solder is in place, heat the joint until the solder flows. There will be a flash of bright silver once the solder has flowed. Remove the flame from the ring immediately. Using copper tongs, carefully remove the piece from the tweezers, drop in warm pickle solution for about five minutes, then rinse with water.

Finishing

11. File any bumps or excess solder from the joint. Excess solder is removed exposing a seamless, continuous ring band.

12. Slide piece onto the ring mandrel. Rest ring mandrel against a secure surface, such as the bench block or ring mandrel hole. Holding the ring mandrel firmly in one hand, swiftly hammer

the ring into shape with a rawhide mallet. Be sure
to flip the ring every few blows to avoid tapering.
Continue hammering the ring with the mallet until
a perfect circle is achieved.

13. To flatten the ring, place the ring on a steel bench
block or anvil and strike with the rawhide mallet,
turning the ring to hammer on both sides until flat.

14. Sand away the file marks and imperfections
caused by shaping using a sanding stick. Start
with coarse-grit paper sticks and move up to fine-
grit sticks, revealing a smooth, bright finish.

15. Sand both sides and all outer surfaces. Sanding
takes time and patience, and the efforts spent
here pay off in the finished piece.

16. A flexible-shaft tool with a split-mandrel bit is used
to sand the inside of the ring. The split mandrel is
a steel rod with a slot cut halfway down the shaft.
Strips of sandpaper can be threaded into the slot
for finishing the inside of curved pieces.

17. Install the bit into the hand piece of the flexible-
shaft tool. Tighten with a chuck key.

18. With the tool set to a slow or medium speed, sand
the inside of the ring, slowly rotating it.

19. Paint the entire ring with black patina solution.
Avoid contact with the solution. Hold the ring with
tweezers while painting the inside, and consider
wearing protective gloves. Patina solution contains hydrochloric acid and it must be washed off
the skin immediately. Rinse and dry the ring and
wash your hands.

20. With a coarse scouring pad, scuff away the surface treatment to reveal a matte finish. Continue
buffing until the desired brightness is achieved.
An alternative to patina is to polish the piece to
a mirror finish on the buffing wheel.

Simple
PROJECT: ## Chased Bangle

This bangle hones the skills learned in the Simple Band Ring (page 91). With basic chasing tools and a hammer, you can create designs, patterns, and textures on the surface of your bracelet. This project teaches chasing designs on a rounded surface, shaping a bracelet on a bracelet mandrel, and using patina to highlight chased designs. With a creative twist and a few extra tools you can create various size bangles that can be stacked, linked together and even chased.

TOOLS

- Flat-nosed pliers
- Scribe
- Jeweler's saw
- Bench block
- Assorted files
- Soldering torch set
- Soldering pick
- Soldering tweezers
- Firebrick
- Flux
- Copper tongs
- Pickle solution
- Sanding sticks
- Scouring pad
- Chasing tools
- Chasing hammer

MATERIALS

- 1 mm × 1.25 mm sterling silver sizing stock (flat or square wire can also be used)
- Sterling silver solder (hard)
- Patina solution

INSTRUCTIONS

Shaping

1. Starting with the wire sizing stock, begin bending the shape by hand. You can use wider or thinner gauge as you prefer. The thicker the metal stock, the more difficult it will be to bend by hand. No matter the width of the metal, the process of creating the bangle is the same.

2. Using your flat-nosed pliers, hold the metal and bend and shape it. Use nylon-jaw pliers, which do not have a serrated pattern cut into the jaws, which will mar and scratch the surface of your work.

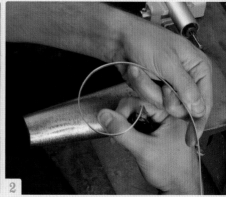

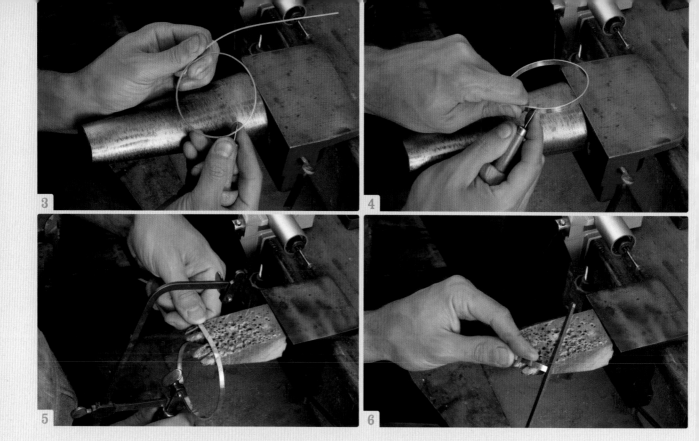

3. Determine the size of the bangle. They may be made smaller for people with small hands or larger for those needing more room. Check the size by attempting to insert your hand through the loop.

4. Once the circular, bangle shape is complete, mark your spot to cut with a sharp scribe. A sharpened steel tool is used here.

5. Place the piece on the jeweler's bench block and cut at your mark with your jeweler's saw. Be sure to cut a straight, flush line. This is important to line up the ends in preparation for soldering. You can use a 2\0 blade for this step.

6. Using a medium- or fine-cut flat file, file both ends of your piece flush. A nice, square end will solder better and require less work than a jagged or tapered joint.

7. Check the ends for fit. Create a spring-like tension on the piece by pushing the ends too far into itself (the ends will overlap as they are forced inward). Once a spring has been created, open the joint back up and line up the ends. The tension on the piece will keep them in place for soldering.

Soldering

8. Solder the joint using hard solder. Use the same soldering technique from the Simple Band Ring project, page 88–91. When finished, place in pickle pot, rinse, and dry.

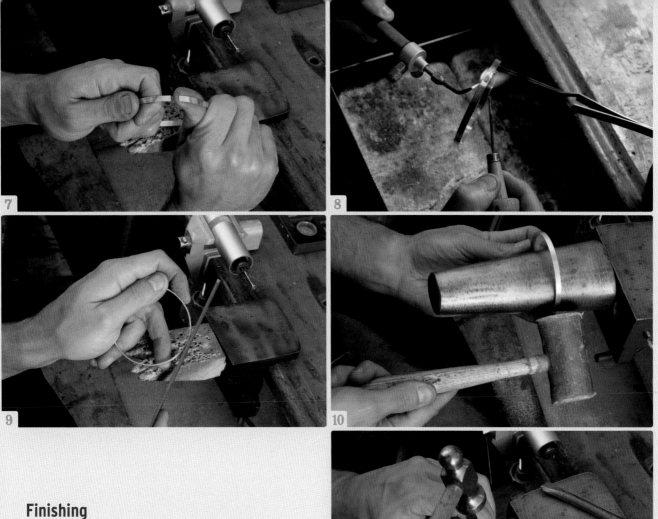

Finishing

9. Using a flat file, remove any additional solder from the joint. Use a long curved motion when filing. Span the whole edge of the bracelet to create a consistent shape. Next, use medium-grit sanding sticks to remove any file marks. Using the same motion, repeat with fine-grit sanding sticks to create a smooth matte finish.

10. You can reshape and straighten the bangle by placing it on the bracelet mandrel. Swift but gentle strikes with the rawhide mallet will help you remove any unwanted bends. Continuously flip and turn the bangle to avoid distorting its shape.

11. Add any patterns or designs using chasing tools. Simply line up the stamping tool and strike with a chasing hammer. Repeat the same pattern or add your own designs. Continue spinning the bangle to complete the design around the entire surface of the metal.

12. You can paint the entire bracelet with black patina solution, being careful not to get any on your skin, then rinse thoroughly with water and dry. Use a scouring pad to scuff away the surface treatment to reveal a matte finish. Continue buffing until the desired brightness is achieved.

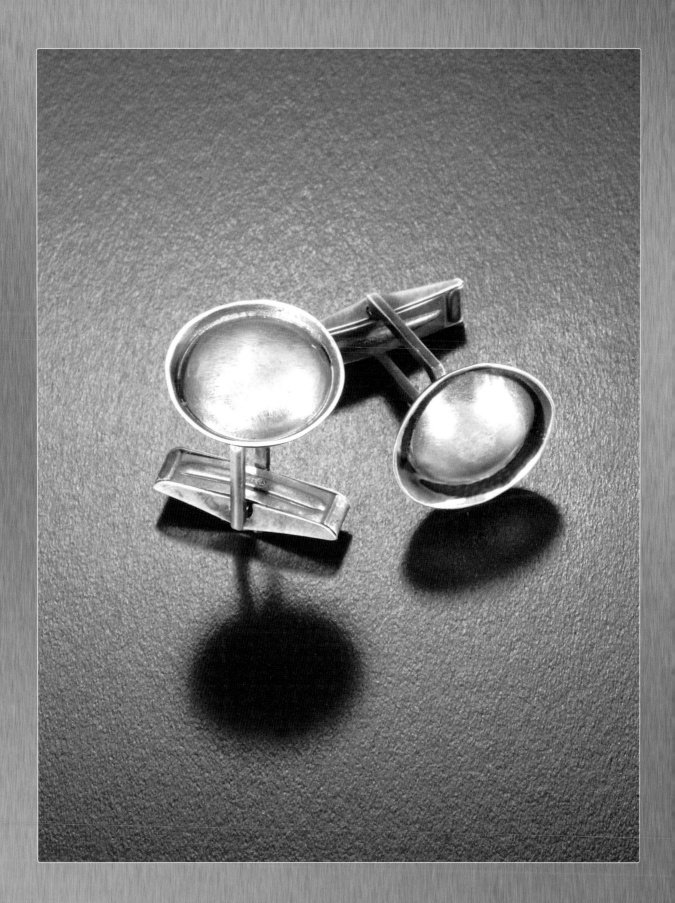

Concave and
PROJECT: # Convex Cufflinks

This project hones soldering techniques and introduces a few important jeweler's tools: the doming block, punches set, and the disc-cutting tool. Cutting symmetrical metal discs and forming them into three-dimensional shapes is essential to building a jewelry repertoire. This project also teaches how to solder findings onto your work. (These techniques can be easily applied to making earrings instead of cufflinks.)

TOOLS

- Disc-cutting tool
- Heavy hammer
- Doming block
- Punches set
- Ball-peen hammer
- Sandpaper
- Drill bit set
- Soldering tweezers
- Flux
- Jeweler's snips
- Firebrick
- Soldering torch set
- Soldering pick
- Copper tongs
- Scouring pad
- Pickle solution

MATERIALS

- 26-gauge sterling silver sheet metal
- Sterling silver sheet solder (hard, medium, and easy)
- Sterling silver cuff link findings
- Black patina solution

INSTRUCTIONS

Shaping

1. Find the largest disc size that your disc cutting tool makes (ideally, the size of a quarter). You will be making two large discs and two medium discs, one of each for both cuff links.

2. With a swift blow from a heavy hammer, strike out the four discs. Your tool should quickly hit the top of the punch square. The tool works best with one swift blow rather than a hammering technique. Always make sure your workbench is stable when striking with a heavy hammer.

3. Here, the largest size discs are struck from the sheet.

4. Using your doming block and punches set, begin making the dome shape in all four parts. Start at the largest dome with the largest punch, slowly working the discs upward using the tool and ball-pein hammer.

5. Work your way up to a more concave or convex shape. These are indicated by a smaller, deeper hole on the doming block. They can eventually become half spheres, but stop just short of that.

6. Here is an example of a good shape. Continue with all four discs.

7. Using a piece of 400-grit sandpaper, sand your discs so they are flush. They will have ripples and flat spots from the tool; they need to be flush for a clean solder joint.

8. It is necessary that you drill a tiny hole in your disc. By placing the medium disc half inside your large disc half, you are creating trapped air in between them. During the soldering process, gasses will build up inside the area and need ventilation through this hole. If you do not drill a vent hole, a small explosion inside could send one of your hot metal discs flying right at you.

Soldering

9. Place one large disc in your soldering tweezers, dome side down. Place a medium size disc dome side up inside. Flux the whole circular joint to be soldered.

10. Cut small squares of hard solder, using your jeweler's snips. Remember to clean your sheet solder either in pickle or with a scouring pad. Tarnished or dirty solder will not flow. Place the chips of solder on the firebrick below your work.

11. Paint your chips of solder with flux. It is better to go heavy on the flux during this step. Once warmed, the flux becomes thick like honey and will work like glue with your soldering pick.

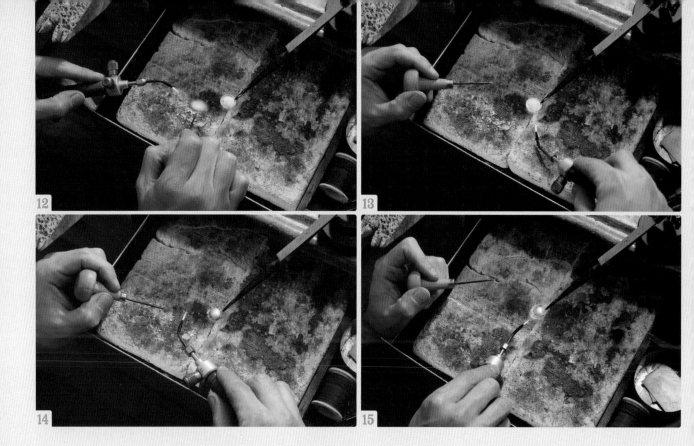

12. Begin heating your chips of solder; they will ball up one by one. Be sure to spread them apart so that they do not ball up together.

13. Warm your piece and begin placing small balls of solder around the perimeter of the joint. Continue picking up balls of solder from the firebrick. You will need to place four or five solder balls all around the joint.

14. Here, the solder is in place and ready to flow.

15. Heat the whole piece with a bushy blue flame until the solder flows. Immediately remove the flame. If you overheat at this step you run the risk of melting your work. Remove the piece with copper tongs and place it in the pickle pot for five minutes. Remove from pickle, rinse, and dry.

16. Insert the piece large dome side up in the soldering tweezers. Paint with flux again to prepare for the next joint. Pick up the sterling cuff link part with a spare set of soldering tweezers. Be sure to flux the end of the cuff link finding as well.

17. Using medium solder chips, begin heating them until they ball up. Then, using your soldering pick, pick up only one. Only a small amount of solder is needed for this next joint.

18. Slowly heat the piece while beginning to position your joint. You will simultaneously be heating both parts while you drop the cuff link finding into place. At the point when the solder flows, quickly remove the heat. Your cuff link finding should now be securely soldered.

19. After soldering, use your copper tongs to place the piece in the pickle pot for about five minutes. The piece shown has been pickled.

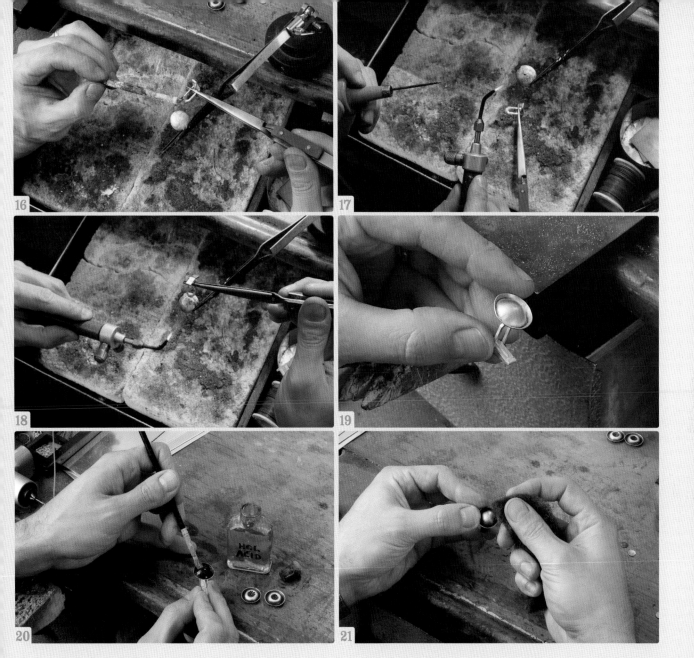

Finishing

20. Completely paint the piece with black patina solution, including the cuff link mechanism and the back. Be careful not to get solution on your skin. Rinse and dry.

21. Using a scouring pad to scuff away the surface treatment to reveal a matte finish. Continue to desired brightness.

22. Repeat steps 9 to 20 for the second cuff.

Riveted
PROJECT: Bead Ring

All jewelers should have cold connections in their skill set. Sometimes soldering may not be possible if the piece's materials cannot tolerate heat. Knowing basic cold connections, such as rivets, will come in handy. This project's design focus is a simple straightforward rivet. Change the focal bead, alter the shape of the ring, modify it to suit your taste: the technique is still the same. Also explored are spacers and flaring your tubing to make round rivet heads.

TOOLS

- Flat-nosed pliers
- Ring mandrel
- Jeweler's saw
- File
- Sanding sticks
- Riveting tool
- Flexible-shaft tool
- Drill bit set
- Riveting hammer
- Split mandrel
- Scouring pad

MATERIALS

- 5 mm × 1.25 mm sterling silver sizing stock (wide flat wire can also be used)
- Medium bead of your choice, as long as the tubing fits through the hole. For this project, a Naga shell bead was used.
- Sterling silver tubing
- Black patina solution

INSTRUCTIONS

Shaping

1. Start by using flat-nosed pliers to bend sizing stock. Note that your piece may look slightly different than the one shown. This project requires a sense of proportion that depends on your focal bead.

2. Shape sizing stock as shown. This project requires a single piece of sizing stock bent to hold your bead of choice.

3. Use a ring mandrel to help you shape the ring shank. At this time decide your size and check it against your sizing stick. Your size will determine the placement of your next bend.

4. After deciding where to bend the shank, test your focal bead for fit. It is fine to return to step 1 and reshape your piece. There is no specific way to measure other than to try it on with the bead in place. You want the correct shape and size before cutting.

5. Using your jeweler's saw, position your work firmly against your bench pin. Cut your sizing stock so both sides of the ring are uniform. Your piece should be a symmetrical stirrup shape.

6. Using a flat, fine-cut file, clean the edges of the piece. If you prefer soft corners, use the file to round them. Use sanding sticks to remove any tool marks left from your pliers.

7. Insert your focal bead into the opening and use it as a guide. Use a riveting tool or scribe to mark your holes for drilling. Be sure to view it from both sides to check for level.

8. Using your flexible-shaft tool, insert a drill bit that is smaller than your desired diameter. Drill out both sides of your ring. You can move up incrementally in size until the holes match your tubing. Test for fit along the way. Your holes should receive the tubing without play. A snug fit is required for this ring.

9. Using a drill bit four to five times larger than your hole, gently twist around the rim removing the burr created from drilling. You can countersink this hole for a tighter fit.

10. With pressure applied to the ring shank, test-fit all of your parts for alignment. Measure the length of tubing you will need to create the rivets. Be sure to leave ample room for flaring of the tubing on either end before marking your cut.

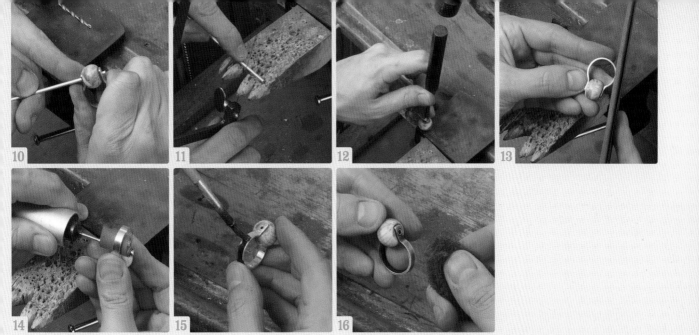

11. Using your jeweler's saw, support the section of tubing against your bench pin and cut at your mark. Move slowly and let the tool do the work. Tubing is sometimes difficult to cut.

12. Carefully hold all of the pieces together and rest on a steel bench block. Using your riveting tool, begin to flare the tubing to create your rivet head. Flip your work over and flare the opposite side at the same rate as the first. Slowly continue to flare each side equally and while holding pressure to the ring shank. Use a riveting hammer to help you when the pressure is too great to flare by hand. Small, gentle taps work better than swift blows.

Finishing

13. Now that your rivet is set, you can clean up any tooling marks using a fine-cut sanding stick. If you're daring, and have countersunk both of your drill holes, you can file and sand away the rivet heads leaving what is called a hidden rivet that will hold your piece just as well. These flush-style rivets are useful for mechanical joints or when a rivet head is not necessary.

14. Using your split mandrel mounted in your flexible-shaft tool, sand the inside of your ring shank to remove tooling marks. Use slow to medium speed or your paper will tear. Do not sand your bead flat on the inside of the shank.

15. Paint the piece with black patina, avoiding the bead. Some materials can be damaged by the corrosive nature of this patina. Always rinse your work and wash your hands.

16. Use a scouring pad to scuff away the surface treatment to reveal a matte finish. Continue to desired brightness.

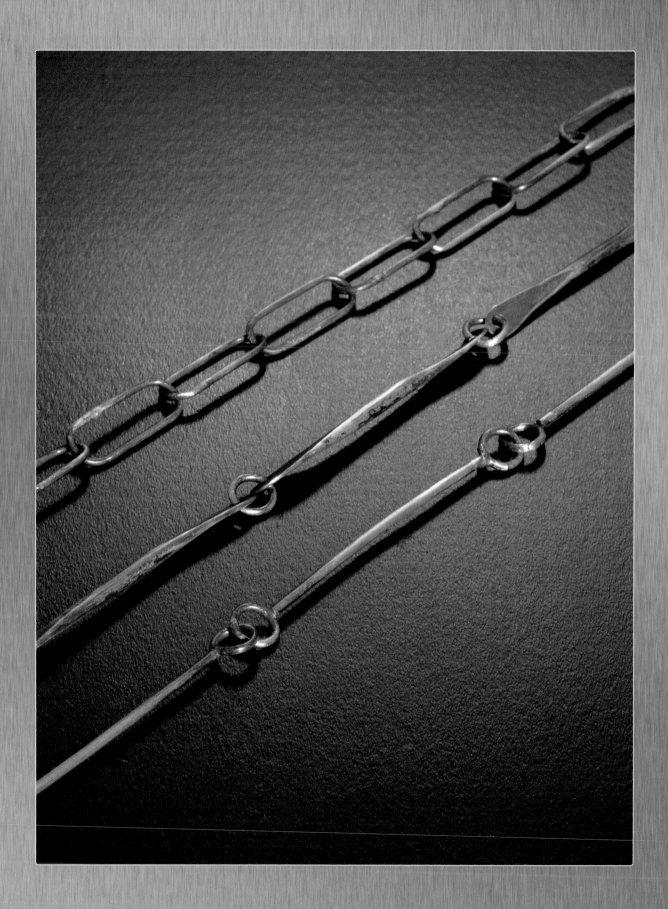

Chain
PROJECT: Making

Incorporating a handmade chain into a necklace design adds personality that cannot be achieved with commercially manufactured chain. This project introduces making jump rings, the most basic chain-making technique and the foundation for many projects. They can be used as bails and connections and can serve many other functions. As these core techniques are honed, they will inspire other unique chain-making ideas and designs.

TOOLS

- Steel jump ring mandrels in various sizes
- Bench pin
- Jeweler's saw
- Side cutters
- File
- Flux
- Soldering torch set
- Soldering tweezers
- Soldering pick
- Firebrick
- Copper tongs
- Round-nosed pliers
- Flat-nosed pliers
- Chasing or silversmith hammer
- Flexible-shaft tool
- Drill bit set
- Steel bench block
- Disposable wooden mandrels such as chopsticks, rulers, and paintbrush handles

MATERIALS

- Sterling silver wire in various gauges
- Sterling silver solder (hard)

INSTRUCTIONS

Example 1

Knowing how to make jump rings is a useful and important skill for the aspiring jeweler. Jump rings are usually made to size for the specific need. They can be made from various sizes of wire in many different gauges and even with different shaped wire such as square. When making jump rings, always make a few extra to have on hand. It's just as time-consuming to make one as it is to make five. Jump rings are the main connection method for most chain. Your jump rings can be various styles to make great-looking chain. This section will cover a few different styles and options for making your own chain, all of which use jump rings made from wire.

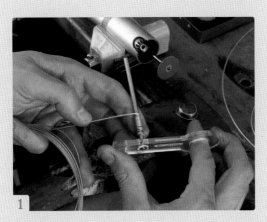

1. Wrap your wire around a mandrel (18-gauge wire works well for this style chain). A coil of about 1 inch (2.5 cm) or so is easy to work with. This handy tool allows you to make various size rings and securely holds the wire end while wrapping around the shaft.

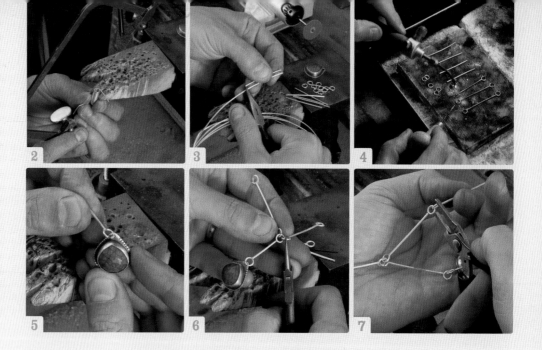

2. Slide the coil off the mandrel and secure it in a groove on your bench pin. Use your jeweler's saw to cut a slit lengthwise up the coil. As each of the rings is cut from the coil, they may collect on your jeweler's saw or fall. Be sure to have your catch tray open.

3. For this style chain, 16-gauge wire is used for the straight sections. Measure each piece about 1½ inches (3.8 cm). Use the first one cut to measure the remaining sections. Cut with side cutters or a jeweler's saw. File each end flush so that there is no angled pointed wire at the end.

4. Set the sections and jump rings on the soldering pad. Line them up so they are ready to be soldered. Solder with hard solder. Be sure to not solder your jump rings closed or you will be unable to attach them. Place each one in the pickle solution for about five minutes.

5. Hook each of the sections together. For a strong chain, be sure to solder the rings closed once attached. A shorter section was made for the pendant drop.

6. Begin connecting the sections as shown. Again, be sure to solder each of the jump rings closed for a strong chain.

7. Use round- or flat-nosed pliers to make the connections. Continue with the pattern to complete the desired length of the chain.

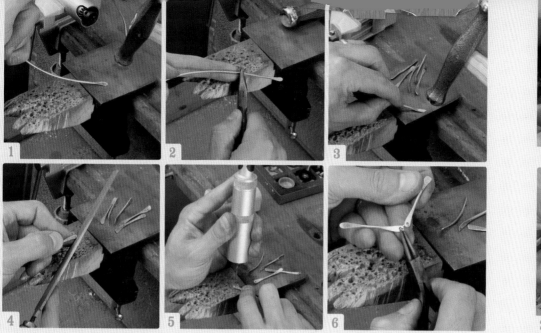

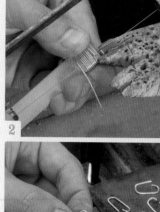

Example 2

This is a different example of chain using jump rings. For this project, heavy-gauge wire was used for the long sections. This style incorporates forging of the wire ends to make a unique design.

1. Using 14-gauge wire, begin flattening the end using the back side of your chasing hammer or a silversmith hammer. Strike with even blows to avoid overstretching any portion of the wire.

2. Cut sections about 1 inch (2.5 cm) each; they will stretch and elongate as you forge them.

3. Repeat the same forging shape on the other end. Make a number of these parts the same way. Chain making involves repeated processes and production-based methods.

4. Round each of the ends using a medium-cut file. This makes each piece uniform in shape.

5. Drill out each end using a larger than necessary bit. For this project, a size 50 drill bit was used.

6. Connect the jump rings to each of your sections and solder them closed. Continue with this pattern until the desired length is reached.

Example 3

1. For elongated jump rings, use a disposable wooden mandrel. For this project, a halved section of ruler was used. You can use any shape your desired jump ring should be as the mandrel. Wrap the wire around the mandrel material for as many rings as needed. One complete wrap makes one jump ring.

2. Either slide the coil off of the mandrel material or, if it is disposable wood, cut into it as shown. Paintbrush handles, chopsticks, and other disposable wood material make for great jump ring mandrel shapes. Cut each of the sections using you jeweler's saw.

3. Once cut, connect them one by one using your round- or flat-nosed pliers, then solder each ring closed for a strong chain.

Chunky
PROJECT: Bead Ring

This ring uses the versatile Simple Band Ring (see page 91) as a foundation, integrating riveting skills learned from the Riveted Bead Ring (see page 102). Any bead of choice can perch on top of the band, just be sure the rivet tubing passes through the bead's hole without much play. Here you learn to make a standard bead cap, which is an elegant finishing touch.

TOOLS

- Disc-cutting tool
- Doming block
- Punches set
- Hammer
- Flat-nosed pliers
- Flexible-shaft tool
- Drill bit set
- Oversized drill bit
- Scribe
- Jeweler's saw
- File
- Ring mandrel
- Third hand
- Jeweler's snips
- Flux
- Soldering torch set
- Soldering tweezers
- Firebrick
- Soldering pick
- Copper tongs
- Pickle solution
- Rawhide mallet
- Bench block or anvil
- Sanding stick
- Flexible-shaft tool
- Slotted sandpaper
- Mandrel bit
- Scouring pad
- Riveting tool
- Riveting hammer

MATERIALS

- 5 mm × 1.25 mm sterling silver sizing stock (wide flat wire can also be used)
- Sterling silver sheet solder (hard and medium)
- Black patina solution
- 26-gauge sterling silver sheet
- Sterling silver tubing
- Faceted large round bead of your choice
- Sterling silver solder (hard)
- Patina solution

INSTRUCTIONS

Shaping

1. Insert the sheet metal into the disc-cutting tool. Select the appropriate size disc for your bead. Swiftly strike the punch to knock out discs from your sheet metal. You will need two of the same size for the top and bottom of your bead. These are called caps.

2. Place your bead caps into the doming block. Doming punches are used to shape the metal into tiny hemisphere shapes. The degree and severity of the dome depend on the size and shape of your doming block and choice of punch. Always start with a slightly domed shape and gradually create sharper domes as you move to smaller punches. Be sure to test-fit your caps on your bead every so often.

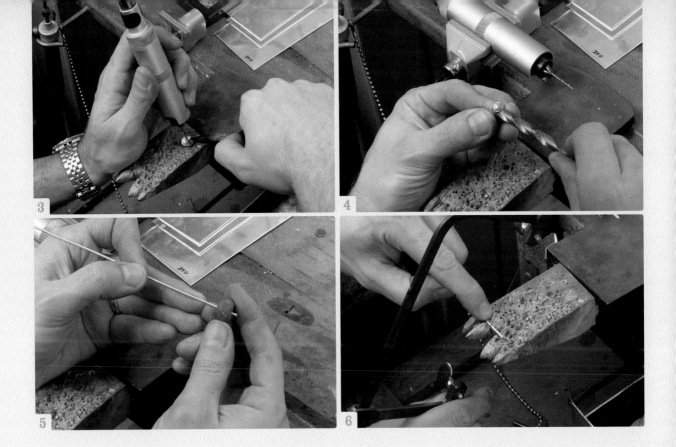

3. Holding your domed cap with pliers, drill out the center using a 2.0 mm bit or the same size bit as your tubing. Do not attempt to hold the cap with your fingers; the sharp edges will cut you if your drill bit grabs your work and begins spinning it. Drill out both bead caps.

4. Clean up the hole by using an oversized drill bit and only hand pressure. A bit five to ten times larger will do. Using light hand pressure, twist the bit around the rim of the hole to countersink it and remove any burrs.

5. Test-fit your tubing to make sure it slides easily through your bead and the caps. Put all of the pieces together on the length of tubing and measure it. Mark your cut with a scribe. Give yourself a little room for the rivet and the solder joint. It is best to cut it too long than too short, as you can always trim it before setting the rivet.

6. Cut your section of tubing at your mark. Cut slowly and let the saw do the work. Tubing can be held in a special tool called a jig. This tool is handy if you need to cut many of the same size pieces of tubing or wire. File the edges flat and prepare it for soldering.

Soldering

7. This project uses a simple band ring. Review how to make a simple band ring on page 91. Place the ring blank in the soldering tweezers. Clean the ring from dirt and oils by dipping it in the pickle pot or by scuffing it with a scouring pad. Paint the area to be soldered with flux.

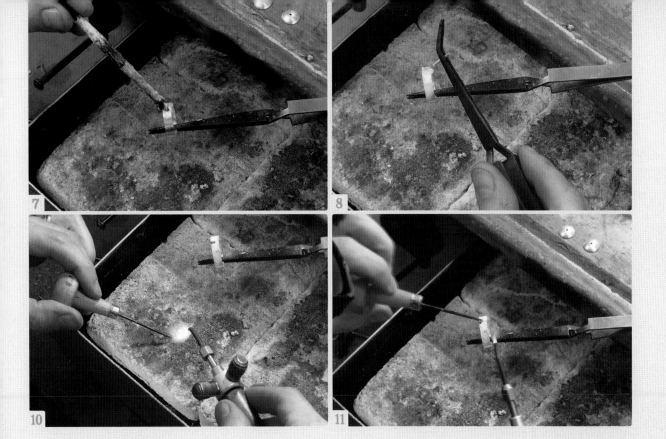

8. Place your cleaned section of tubing in a spare set of soldering tweezers. Be sure not to touch it with your fingers. Dirt and oils from your skin will prevent the flow of solder. Paint the tubing with flux too.

9. Cut small squares of medium solder from your sheet. (See Simple Band Ring, step 8, page 90.) Make sure your solder is clean and not tarnished (a quick scuff with a scouring pad works great). Place the squares on the soldering block or firebrick below your work piece. Flux the chips of solder. At this step hard solder is used for your ring blank while medium solder will be used for the next solder joint. If you were to solder this piece later, use easy solder to prevent flowing of your previous solder joints.

10. Prepare your solder joint by balling up a few of your fluxed chips on the firebrick. Carefully pick them up with your soldering pick and place them on the joint. This process is called sweat soldering.

11. Prepare the area around the joint by warming it gently. Once your solder is in place, heat it until it flows, then pull the flame away quickly creating a small pool of solder. This prepares the joint for the next step. Keep the piece warm but not to the point of melting your solder again.

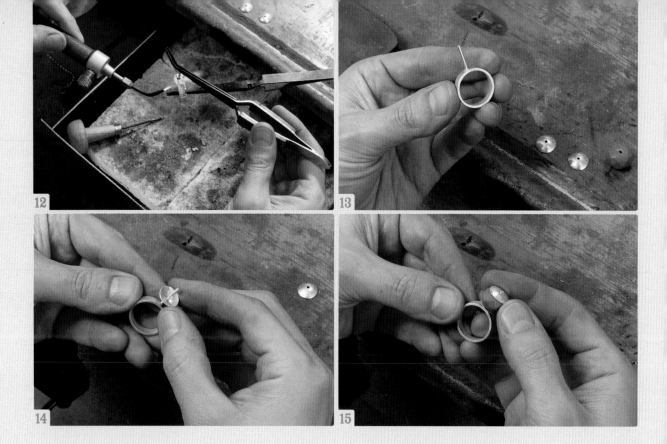

12. Pick up your soldering tweezers that are holding the section of tubing. Bring them into the flame and close to the solder joint. While keeping the entire piece warm, position your tubing and heat to the point that your solder flows. At that point, drop the tubing into place and quickly remove the flame. Overheating at this stage will melt your tubing. The joint should now be soldered.

13. After soldering, pickle your work piece for about five minutes. Then rinse with water and dry. Now you have the shaft that will hold your bead and caps.

Finishing

14. Assemble your pieces. First slide the bottom cap on the shaft. It may be necessary to twist the cap slightly while pushing it on. If the cap will not fit, try redrilling with a slightly larger bit.

15. Next, slide the bead onto the shaft and complete with the top cap. You should see a small section of tubing extending from the top cap that will be used to flare the tubing that will create the holding rivet. If you have more than what is shown, remove your parts and trim to size.

16. Place your piece on a ring mandrel. Slide it all the way up on the mandrel so it is secure. While firmly holding the ring shank and your piece, use your riveting tool to begin flaring the tubing. Use circular motions to slowly work the metal outward. You may want to put a little pressure downward on your bead and cap to create tension that will hold it all together.

17. While still firmly holding your work, begin tapping the end of the flared tubing down uniformly. Use rotating taps all around the edges of the tubing continually flaring the rivet. The pressure that this creates will hold your caps and bead securely.

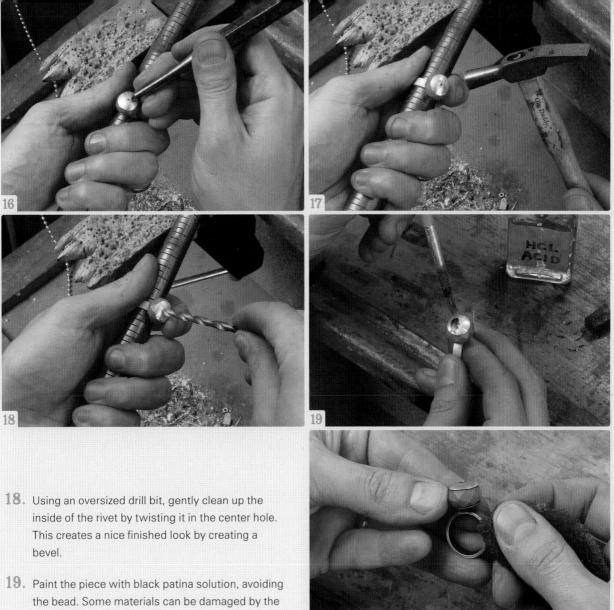

18. Using an oversized drill bit, gently clean up the inside of the rivet by twisting it in the center hole. This creates a nice finished look by creating a bevel.

19. Paint the piece with black patina solution, avoiding the bead. Some materials can be damaged by the corrosive nature of this patina. Always rinse your work and wash your hands.

20. Use a scouring pad to scuff away the surface treatment to reveal a matte finish. Continue to desired brightness.

Bezel-Set
PROJECT: **Pendant**

Bezel setting is a core jeweler's technique that is fun, simple to learn, with endless possibilities. Any stone or cabochon with a flat back and soft rounded edges can be bezel set—the shape does not matter. This project is versatile and there are endless spins to be put on it even while dabbling in the basic techniques. Here, you are introduced to a few more specialty tools, such as a bezel pusher and a burnishing tool. This pendant uses your soldering skills as well, as it emphasizes the importance of well-fitting joints.

TOOLS

- Scribe
- Jeweler's saw
- Fine file
- Flat-nosed pliers
- Third hand
- Flux
- Soldering torch set
- Soldering tweezers
- Soldering pick
- Firebrick
- Copper tongs
- Pickle solution
- Sandpaper
- Sanding sticks
- Flexible-shaft tool
- Drill bit set
- Square bezel pusher
- Burnisher
- Scouring pad
- Buffing wheel

MATERIALS

- Fine silver bezel wire
- 22-gauge sterling silver sheet metal
- Sterling silver sheet solder (hard)
- Faceted stone of your choice (for this project, chrysocola was used)
- Patina solution

INSTRUCTIONS

Shaping

1. Measure the circumference of the stone with your bezel wire. Wrap the wire all the way around and allow the ends to overlap.

2. Mark the metal for your cut using a scribe or other sharp object. Try to be as accurate as possible. A bezel that is cut too small can sometimes be stretched, but a bezel that is too large must be resoldered.

3. Cut your bezel wire using a jeweler's saw; never cut with side cutters. The saw makes a flush, square end on the wire that is needed for soldering.

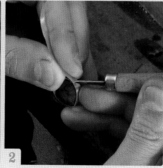

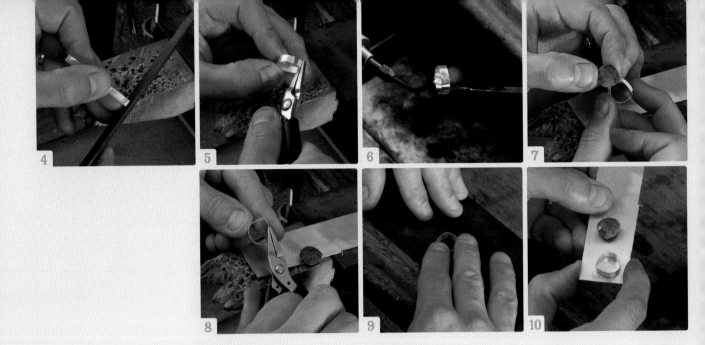

4. File the ends flush and flat like a square. They should make a seamless joint with no gaps.

5. Using your flat-nosed pliers, close the bezel so that it has a spring to it. The tension created by the spring should keep your ends touching flush during the solder joint. Again, soldering is about preparation.

Soldering

6. Place the piece in the third hand tweezers and paint with flux. Solder the joint using hard solder. Using copper tongs, remove from the tweezers and place in the pickle solution for about five minutes.

7. Test fit the stone in place.

8. Using flat-nosed pliers, correct the shape. Test-fit the stone in place again. If the stone does not pass easily through the wire, then attempt to stretch with flat-nosed pliers. If it appears too large, cut and resolder.

9. Place the piece on a flat surface with fine sandpaper. Just a few swipes will remove any ridges and high spots making the piece flat all the way around.

10. Check to make sure the bezel is flat by placing it on your metal. No gaps should be seen anywhere around the joint.

11. Place the piece in the third hand tweezers, paint with flux then solder with medium solder. Using copper tongs, remove from the tweezers and place in the pickle solution for about five minutes. Rinse with water and dry.

Finishing

12. Using your jeweler's saw, cut out the shape leaving a little extra metal all the way around the bezel wall. This lip can be any shape you desire.

13. File the burr edges from the saw blade using a fine file. Then use sanding sticks to remove the file marks and soften the sharp edges.

14. Drill out a hole for the chain using your flexible-shaft tool.

15. A design pattern is created using the jeweler's saw. Small incisions are cut repeatedly around the entire edge of the piece for subtle texture.

16. Place the stone in the bezel cup.

17. Set in place using your square bezel pusher tool. Crimp the bezel around the stone equally from all sides. This pinching process creates the holding tension that keeps the stone secure. Do not push too hard on one side or the stone will not sit flat.

18. Smooth out any bumps, ripples, and ridges using the burnishing tool. This tool creates an additional lip of metal that touches the stone and keeps it from rattling.

19. Paint with patina solution, avoiding the stone. Some stones will discolor with harsh chemicals. Rinse with cool water and dry.

20. Use a scouring pad to finish to desired brightness. Polishing on the buffing wheel will produce a brilliant, shiny surface.

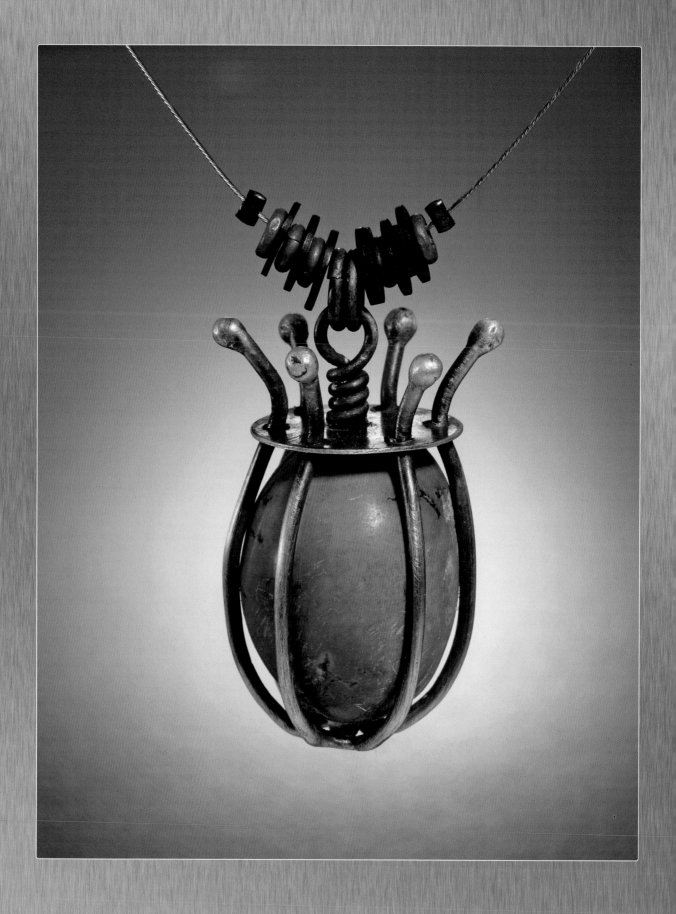

PROJECT: Cage Pendant

This project teaches a basic enclosure, the cage, which can be made to fit your object precisely. This simple cage can be modified to accommodate any shape or size object you may have. For this project, a large piece of turquoise was used. This pendant applies basic soldering skills, measuring, and heat treatments as well as wire-working.

TOOLS

- Side cutters
- Various files
- Firebrick
- Soldering pick
- Soldering tweezers
- Soldering torch set
- Flux
- Copper tongs
- Pickle solution
- Flat-nosed pliers
- Disc-cutting tool
- Hammer
- Sandpaper
- Dividers
- Flexible-shaft tool
- Drill bit set
- Smooth-jaw flat-nosed pliers
- Round-nosed pliers
- Scouring pad

MATERIALS

- 16-, 18-, and 20-gauge sterling silver wire
- 26-gauge sterling silver sheet metal
- Jump ring
- Sterling silver sheet solder (hard)
- Stone or object of your choice (green-yellow turquoise was used for this project)
- Patina solution

INSTRUCTIONS

Cutting

1. Cut six sections of 16-gauge wire about 2 inches (5.1 cm) long using side cutters.

2. File the ends flush and flat using a fine-cut file.

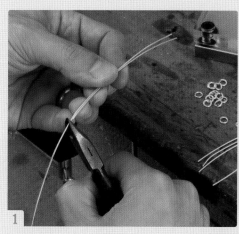

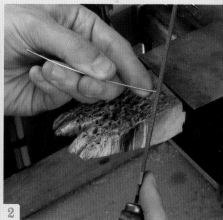

Soldering

3. Start assembling the bottom of the cage on the firebrick or soldering pad. Use a pick and tweezers to make sure the spacing is equal all the way around. A jump ring is used for the center.

4. Solder all the joints using hard solder. Be sure to have a good solid connection and no weak joints. Using copper tongs, place in pickle solution for about five minutes, rinse, and dry.

Shaping

5. Begin shaping the cage using flat-nosed pliers. Carefully bend each of the sections as shown.

6. Cut a disc of metal from 26-gauge sheet for the top. Depending on the size of your stone, your disc may need to be smaller or larger.

7. Once the disc has been filed and sanded smooth, use dividers to mark equal drill holes all the way around the edge of the disc.

8. Drill the holes using your flexible-shaft tool. Select a drill bit size slightly larger than your wire. You need a little wiggle room for the wire to be passed through.

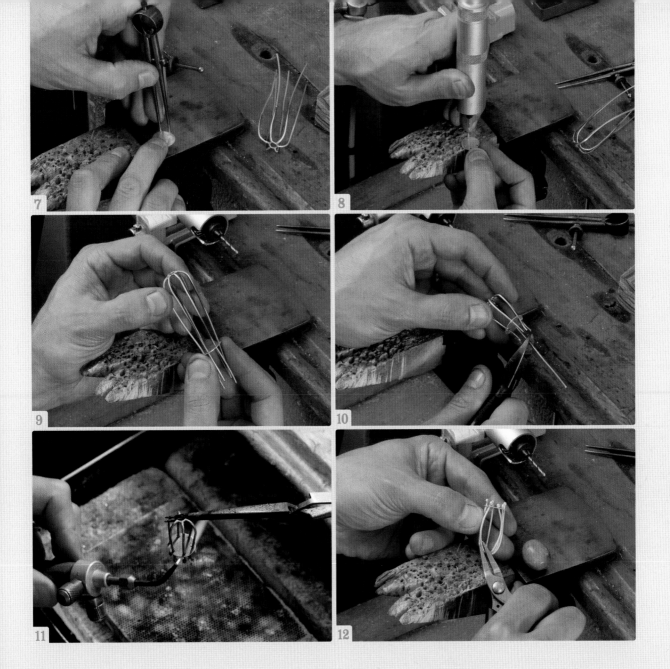

9. Push the wire ends through the holes in the disc as shown.

10. Trim the wire to size using side cutters.

11. Use your torch to heat the ends of the wire until they begin to ball up. Be sure to create balls about the same size and length as the rest.

12. Spread the bars open enough to pass your object through. Use smooth-jaw flat-nosed pliers so that you do not mar or scratch the wire.

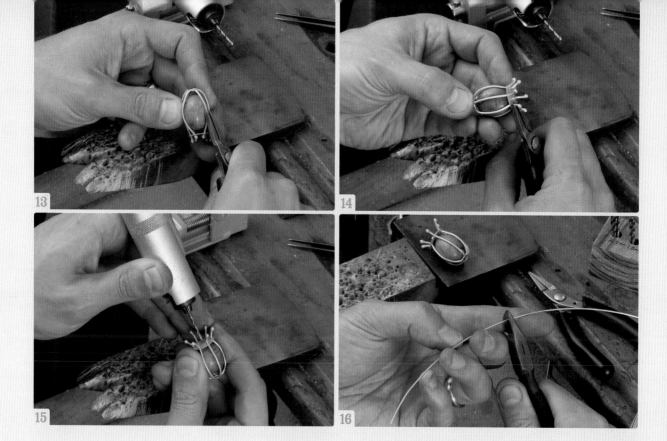

13. Place the object inside and bend the bars back in place.

14. Bend the ends of wire back slightly, this creates the tension needed to secure your object and prevent rattling.

15. Drill a hole in the end disc if your object is a bead to allow for a headpin to be inserted.

16. Cut a section of 20- or 22-gauge wire for your headpin.

17. Ball up the end of the wire using your torch.

18. Pass the headpin wire through the entire piece.

19. Begin making your bail using round-nosed pliers.

20. A loop and wrap technique is sufficient for closure.

21. A simple coil wire wrapped around the shaft is used. Trim away any excess.

22. Attach a jump ring. When suspended, this extra ring allows for swinging and kinetic movement.

Finishing

23. Paint with patina solution, rinse with cool water then dry. Use a scouring pad to finish to desired brightness.

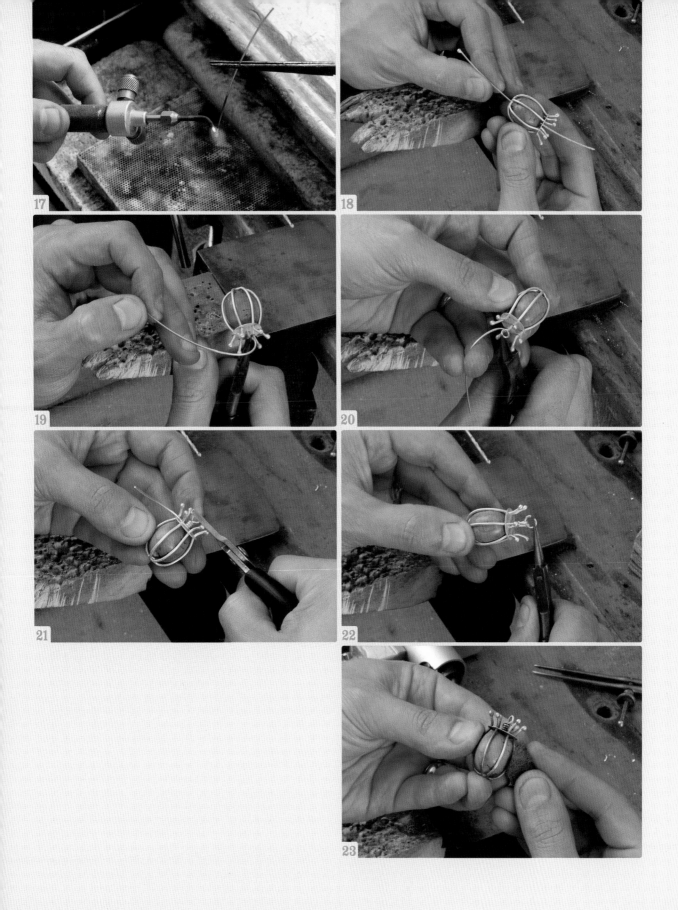

Open-Band
PROJECT: Copper Bracelet

Expand your shaping skills with the bracelet mandrel and create a simple hinge that incorporates a focal bead into the bracelet design. One simple solder joint, basic metal forming skills, and an eye for color harmonize in this piece. The Peruvian opal is offset to create a deliberately asymmetrical look.

TOOLS

- Scouring pad
- Flat-nosed pliers
- Scribe
- Jeweler's saw
- Assorted files
- Sandpaper
- Flexible-shaft tool
- Drill bit set
- Soldering tweezers
- Firebrick
- Soldering torch set
- Copper tongs
- Flux
- Soldering pick
- Pickle solution
- Sanding stick
- Bracelet mandrel
- Rawhide mallet

MATERIALS

- 18- or 20-gauge copper sheet metal
- 22-gauge sterling round wire
- 18-gauge sterling flat wire
- Sterling silver sheet solder (hard)
- Stone of your choice
- Patina solution

INSTRUCTIONS

Shaping

1. Start with your desired width piece of copper sheet metal. For this project, 18-gauge copper sheet was cut into a ¾ × 8 inch (1.9 × 20.3 cm) piece. You can use whatever size works best for your wrist. The copper was cleaned with a scouring pad until it had a bright finish.

2. Using your flat-nosed pliers, bend 18-gauge flat wire to create a holding mechanism. This brace will act like a hinge suspending the stone in place with a pin. The stone used for this project was an oval, cushion-cut Peruvian opal. It was drilled lengthwise to use as a bead.

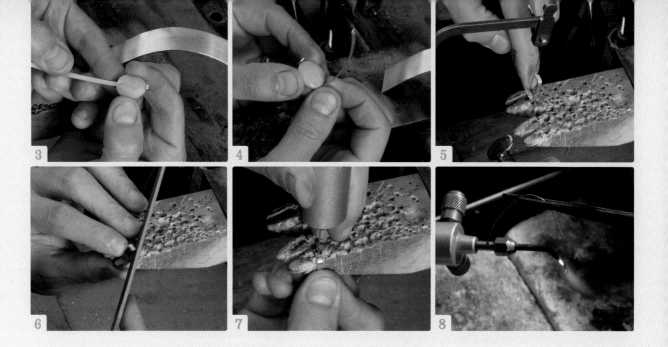

3. Check for size of the stone. Decide where your next bend should be and mark with a scribe.

4. Bend again on the other side of the stone using your flat-nosed pliers. Now you are checking for fit and to determine your mark for cutting. Once decided, score your mark for cutting using a scribe.

5. Cut at your mark using your jeweler's saw. You should have a clean, straight cut. This part will be the brace for your stone. It should look like a crisp bracket symbol ( ]).

6. Using a fine-cut flat file, round the corners of your piece to soften the sharp edges. Once soldered in place, the corners will face out. If they are not filed and sanded to soft edges they may scratch or snag on the wearer's skin and clothes.

7. Using your flexible-shaft tool, drill holes in both end tabs. Select the appropriate size drill bit to match your wire pin. For this project, 22-gauge wire was used for the pin, so a size 56 drill bit was used to drill the holes. Make sure they line up with the stone's holes. Test for fit.

8. Cut a section of 22-gauge wire with a jeweler's saw to make your pin. Place this piece of wire in the soldering tweezers. With your torch, use a bushy blue flame to heat the ends of the wire. Once the metal becomes red and begins to ball up, remove the flame. Remove from tweezers using copper tongs and quench in cool water.

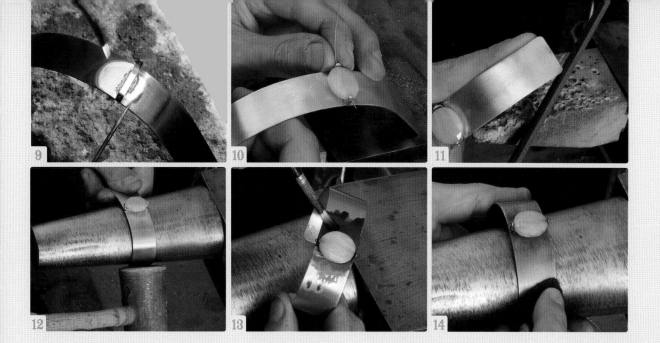

Soldering

9. Solder your bracket part in place using hard solder. For this project, the part was intentionally soldered asymmetrically. Make sure your part is soldered with even spacing on either side and in a straight line. Try heating from underneath and use a pick to move your part into place. Once soldered, place it in the pickle pot for about five minutes, then rinse and dry.

Finishing

10. Place the stone in the bracket and insert the pin as shown. Once in place, trim the pin using nippers at about a ¼ inch (6 mm). Heat again with the torch to ball up the other end of the pin; be sure to not heat the stone directly or it will crack.

11. Soften the corners and edges of the entire bracelet using a fine-cut file. Go over all the areas a second time with a sanding stick to remove the file marks. Rounding the corners makes for a comfortable fit when wearing.

12. Shape the bracelet on the mandrel. Using a raw-hide mallet, gently tap and bend the metal around the shape. If using a tapered mandrel like the one shown, flip the bracelet every so often so the bracelet does not take on the tapered shape.

13. Paint the bracelet with a patina solution. This piece was painted with an acid-based chemical to darken the copper. Wear protection and wash your hands and the work piece with warm water.

14. Gently scratch the surface with a scouring pad. Finish to the desired brightness.

PROJECT: Chunky Stone Ring

This chunky ring taps into skills gleaned from many styles of projects: soldering, bezel setting, measuring, creating good-fitting joints, and metal-forming techniques. For this project, serrated bezel wire was used, adding a subtle design element, with large, milky agate stone for the cabochon.

TOOLS

- Scribe
- Jeweler's saw
- Files (coarse, medium, and fine)
- Various grades of sandpaper
- Third hand
- Soldering torch set
- Soldering tweezers
- Flux
- Soldering pick
- Copper tongs
- Pickle solution
- Flat-nosed pliers
- Soldering tripod with steel mesh screen
- Sanding sticks (coarse, medium, and fine)
- Ring mandrel
- Flexible-shaft tool
- Sanding disc bit
- Bench pin
- Burnisher
- Scouring pad

MATERIALS

- 3" × 3" (7.6 × 7.6 cm) piece of flat 20-gauge sterling silver sheet metal
- 6" (15.2 cm) -long piece of serrated fine silver bezel wire
- 6" (15.2 cm) -long piece of 1 mm × 1.25 mm ring sizing stock
- Cabochon stone of choice (agate was used for this project)
- Sterling silver solder (hard, medium, and easy)
- Patina solution

INSTRUCTIONS

Shaping

1. Measure the outside circumference of your stone with the serrated bezel wire. Completely wrap it around the edge to prepare to mark your cut. It is fine to err on the side of short rather than too long. Bezel wire can be stretched slightly to accommodate an incorrectly measured cut.

2. Mark your cut using a sharp scribe. A light scratch in the surface of the metal will do. Just push hard enough so you can see your mark with the bare eye.

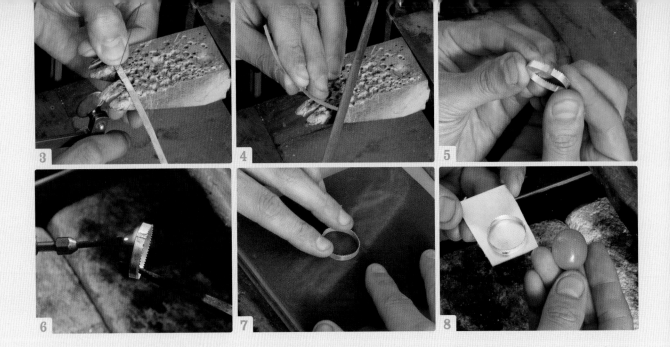

3. Cut the bezel wire using your jeweler's saw. Be sure to cut a clean, straight line. This will help achieve a solid joint during soldering.

4. File the edges of the bezel wire flat and flush. Do not taper the ends. This is also important to achieve a near seamless joint during soldering.

5. Test-fit the edges together and create a spring-like tension to keep the ends touching during soldering. Make sure the edges touch all the way down the seam. Refile and sand if they do not create a solid joint.

Soldering

6. Place the piece in the third hand as shown and solder the joint using hard solder. Use a bushy blue flame and be sure to remove the heat as soon as the solder flows or risk melting the work. Using copper tongs, place the piece in the pickle solution for about five minutes then rinse with water.

7. To prepare this part for soldering, you will need to straighten it with flat-nosed pliers and shape it to the stone exactly. A few gentle swipes on a flat sandpaper sheet should make the bottom seam fit well.

8. In order to get a fluid, solid joint during the next soldering step, test-fit the bezel on the flat sheet metal. Lay the piece on the sheet and look for high spots. A high spot is an area of the bezel that does not touch the sheet metal. You can continue sanding or straightening with pliers until all gaps are removed and the bezel rests flush against the sheet metal.

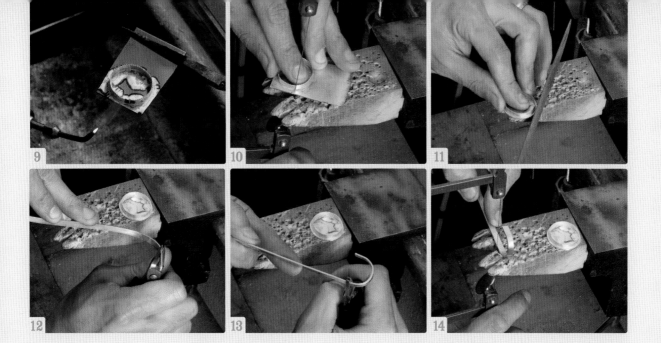

9. Place the work in the third hand as shown. You can also use a soldering tripod with a steel mesh screen if you wish. Solder the joint with medium solder. You want to see a bright flash of silver fluid run the entire distance of the joint. The joint is the entire circle. Make sure your solder flows all the way around. You can place chips separated by a few millimeters all along the circumference of the joint. Place in pickle solution for about five minutes.

10. Using your jeweler's saw, cut the section from the sheet metal. For this project, a millimeter or two has been added all around the edge of the bezel. You can cut it flush or create this lip as well.

11. File away the saw marks and create an even edge. A coarse, flat file is used first, then a medium file, and finally sanding sticks are used to sand the entire edge smooth.

12. Using your flat-nosed pliers, begin shaping the ring shank. (This process requires strong hands to move such thick metal.) Use a steel ring mandrel to help you create the shape.

13. The shape will become a U. Test-fit for size along the way using your ring mandrel. Then score your piece for cutting using a sharp scribe.

14. Cut the section using your jeweler's saw. Be sure to cut a flush straight line again. This is important as well for the next soldering joint.

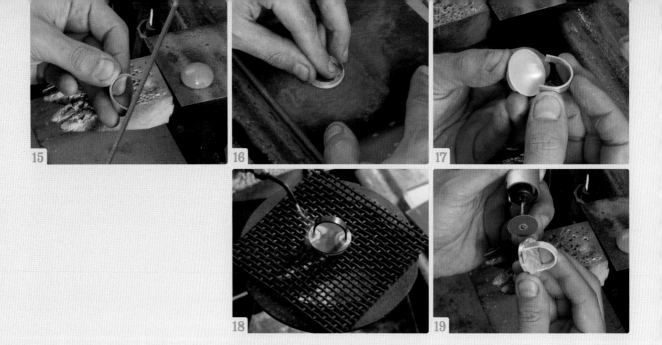

15. Using a flat file, plumb the edges of the ring shank to be sure they are flush with one another. They will need to touch the bezel cup part with no gaps for a strong joint during the next soldering step.

16. Prepare both sides of the joint for soldering using sandpaper. Make sure the ring shank is flat and flush with the cup. Be sure the cup is flat and flush. Use the flat sandpaper to remove any high or low spots. If you place the sandpaper on a piece of glass, you are guaranteed to get a flat surface.

17. Continue to test-fit the parts for a good joint. Again, make sure there are no gaps, that the size is correct, and the parts are level.

18. Place the work on a soldering tripod with a steel mesh screen. A tripod allows you to heat from all areas with your torch. Solder the last joints with easy solder. Be sure to remove the flame once the solder has flowed or risk the earlier joint's solder to reflow. Place in pickle solution for about five minutes then rinse.

Finishing

19. If you have any unsightly solder bumps or ridges, you can clean them up using files or a sanding disc bit inserted in your flexible-shaft tool.

20. Clean up the entire surface area of the ring by removing lips, ridges, and other areas using files and sanding sticks. You want the entire surface area of the ring to be smooth with a matte finish.

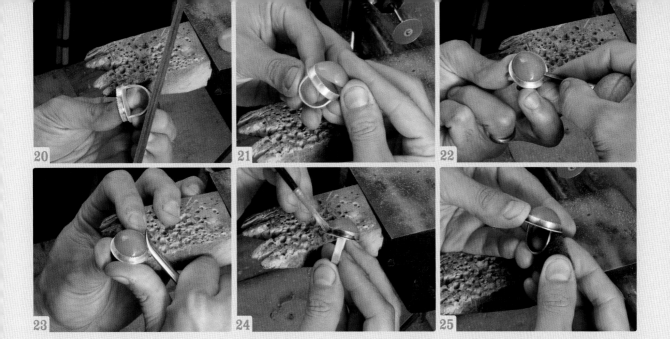

21. Once the ring is finished, the stone can be set. Place the stone in the bezel cup. Gently push it into place. It should fit snugly without being tight. Ideally, the stone should fit perfectly with no rattles or stretched areas. Caution: once pushed into place, the stone cannot be removed!

22. Begin setting by pushing the bezel against the stone using a bezel pusher tool. Work from all sides equally. Moving inward with the tool, use a rocking motion to seal the entire bezel flush against the stone.

23. Remove any ridges and bumps from the bezel pusher with a burnisher. This tool is held and used similar to a potato peeler. It is slid across the surface of the bezel to create a smooth, tooled finish. The burnisher is working when the metal appears polished.

24. Paint the entire piece with patina solution, avoiding the stone. Some minerals cannot tolerate the corrosive nature of patina solutions and therefore begin to deteriorate or discolor. Paint all metal areas except the inside of the ring shank as this patina may irritate the wearer's fingers. Rinse well with water and wash your hands.

25. Finish the ring to the desired brightness with a scouring pad. Brush the surfaces to reveal a bright silver matte finish.

PROJECT: Glass Brooch

This unique project teaches a great mechanism, the spring pin back latch. This piece also incorporates reclaimed or recycled materials and working with glass, and hones soldering and bezel-setting skills. Creating a simple brooch from a watch crystal is a fun way to create a shadowbox. Use your imagination to add various materials and objects to showcase them behind glass.

TOOLS

- Scribe or permanent marker
- Jeweler's saw
- Various files
- Sandpaper
- Flat-nosed pliers
- Soldering tweezers
- Flux
- Soldering torch set
- Soldering pick
- Firebrick
- Copper tongs
- Pickle solution
- Soldering tripod with steel mesh screen
- Sanding sticks
- Cross-locking soldering tweezers
- Flexible-shaft tool
- Sanding disc bit
- Round-nosed pliers
- Bezel pusher
- Burnisher
- Scouring pad

MATERIALS

- 20-gauge sterling silver sheet metal
- 6" (15.2 cm) length of 16-gauge sterling silver wire
- 6" (15.2 cm) length of fine silver bezel wire
- Sterling silver sheet solder (hard)
- Watch crystal or lens of desired shape or size
- Tin lid or object to be set behind glass

INSTRUCTIONS

Shaping

1. Wrap the bezel wire around the circumference of the glass watch crystal. Be sure to keep a snug fit to prepare to mark your cut. Mark your cut with a scribe or permanent marker.

2. Cut the bezel wire using your jeweler's saw. A clean, flush, and square end will aid in preparation for soldering.

3. File and sand the ends of the bezel wire to create square edges. Do not taper the ends. This is important for a strong joint.

4. Begin shaping the metal using flat-nosed pliers so that the ends butt up against each another. The circular shape does not have to be perfect at this time, just as long as the joint is flush and flat.

Soldering

5. Place the piece in the soldering tweezers and prepare the joint for soldering by painting it with flux.

6. Solder the joint using hard solder. Using copper tongs, place the piece in pickle for five minutes.

7. Clean up any solder bumps using a fine file and begin shaping the piece to fit the glass.

8. Once test-fitted on the glass, begin preparing for the next solder joint. Set the bezel on the sheet metal to test for high spots or gaps. The circular bezel should rest on the sheet with the entire face touching the sheet. Sand away any gaps or high spots on a flat surface and retest.

9. Prepare this joint for soldering by painting with flux. Paint both the bezel and the sheet.

10. Be sure to paint all parts with flux inside and out.

11. Place the work on a soldering tripod with a steel mesh screen. Heat from underneath with a hot flame. The steel screen will absorb most of the heat from the flame, so use a sharp, hot flame when soldering this joint. Solder with medium solder. Once a bright fluid ring of solder has flowed around the entire circle, remove with copper tongs and place in pickle for about five minutes.

12. Cut the shape out from the sheet metal using your jeweler's saw. You may cut flush against the bezel to create a cup shape or you can leave a lip around the edge by cutting about a millimeter or two from the bezel wall.

13. File the edge smooth with a coarse file. This removes any bumps and ridges from the saw. Then go over it again with a fine file and finish with sanding sticks until smooth.

14. Using side cutters, cut a 4 to 6 inch (10.2 to 15.2 cm) section of 16-gauge wire to make the pin mechanism for the brooch. File the edges flush and flat.

15. Prepare your surfaces for soldering with sandpaper. Be sure the flat back of the bezel cup is smooth and free of ridges. Sand on a flat surface.

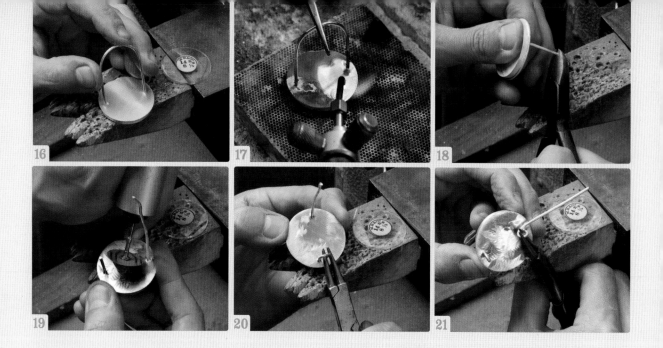

16. Check to be sure your parts fit well with their size, joints, and location.

17. Hold the wire with cross-locking soldering tweezers, and solder with easy solder on a firebrick. Use copper tongs to pick up piece from the firebrick and place in pickle for about five minutes.

Finishing

18. Cut the U shape at one side, leaving enough room for a pin to be made and a latch to be shaped.

19. Clean up any solder bumps or ridges with a sanding disc and your flexible-shaft tool.

20. Shape the catch portion of the pin-back mechanism using round-nosed pliers. A simple half circle should do.

21. Create a spring-like loop in the pin wire end. This allows for tension to be created in the mechanism. The act of making the loop with the round-nosed pliers actually work hardens the metal and makes it spring.

22. Measure where the wire will end at the catch portion of the brooch; do not extend the pin beyond the catch. Cut so that just a millimeter or so of pin wire needs to catch.

23. File the wire to a sharp point. Use files to round and taper the end. Once the shape is attained, finish off the file marks using sanding sticks until a smooth matte finish is achieved.

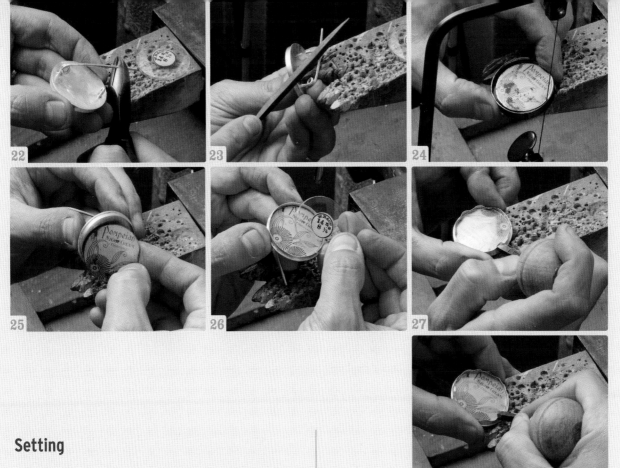

Setting

24. Begin cutting or preparing your material to be inserted and set. For this project, an antique cosmetic tin lid was used.

25. Insert the object as shown. Be sure the size is correct. Once snapped in place, it will be difficult to remove without damaging your piece.

26. Place the glass watch crystal over your item. This must not fit too snug. It cannot rattle but must not be under pressure by the bezel or it may crack.

27. Begin setting the glass by gently bending the bezel around the glass. Be careful not to exert too much force or you risk cracking the glass. The fine silver bezel wire is soft and does not require a lot of pressure to be moved.

28. Finish setting with a burnisher around the outer edge of the bezel. Depending on the materials used, it may not be advisable to paint with a patina solution. Water may collect behind the glass when rinsing, so it is best not to get the piece wet. Create a bright matte finish with a scouring pad.

No-Solder
PROJECT: **Bracelet**

For those who may shy away from using the torch, this no-solder project teaches that you don't always need to use conventional methods for solving a design problem. This solution can be applied to many different styles of jewelry. You will learn basic piercing techniques, including folding and tabbing, which are essential, versatile cold connections.

TOOLS

- Scribe
- Jeweler's saw
- Clamp
- Bench pin
- File
- Sanding sticks
- Ruler
- Flexible-shaft tool
- Drill bit set
- Flat-nosed pliers
- Mini files in various shapes
- Flat-needle file
- Rawhide mallet
- Bracelet mandrel
- Chasing hammer
- Staking tool

MATERIALS

- 22-gauge sterling silver sheet metal

INSTRUCTIONS

1. Score your metal with a scribe or marker. Make a strip about 1 × 7 inches (2.5 × 17.8 cm).

2. Cut the section using your jeweler's saw. A clamp on your bench pin helps secure your work when cutting. A nice straight cut is needed. Follow your line either on one side or the center.

3. Once your section is cut, file the burr edges using a medium-cut file. Remove any ridges, ripples, and sharp sections left from the file. Once filed, go over the entire piece with sanding sticks to remove the file mars and soften the sharp edges.

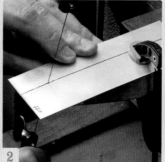

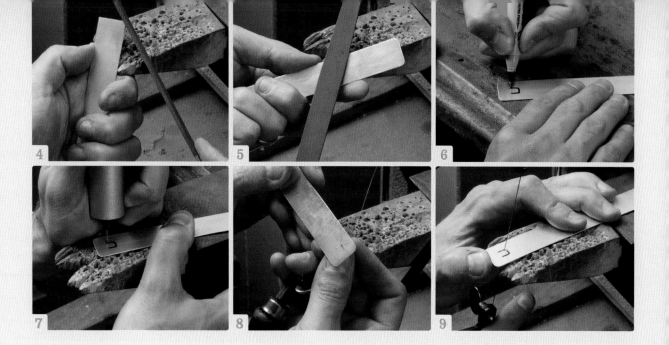

4. File the corners round. This makes for a comfort-able fit when wearing and prevents snagging on clothing. Sharp edges and corners are never desired on jewelry!

5. Continue finishing the entire bracelet. Remove saw marks, file marks, and scratches.

6. Mark the square cutouts using a scribe or marker. Each hole should be 10 × 10 mm square.

7. Drill pilot holes to pass the saw blade through at the corners. Use a drill bit just large enough for the saw blade to fit, no larger.

8. Pass the blade through the hole and connect back to your saw frame. Keep the top of the blade clamped in your frame. Once inserted, clamp the bottom of the blade back into the frame.

9. Cut out your square. Be sure to cut carefully and precisely.

10. Lift the tab using flat-nosed pliers. Create a bend in the tab that allows for a slide latch mechanism to be created. The bend should only be the thick-ness of the sheet metal.

11. Clean up the inside of the cut using needle files. These will remove sharp burrs and shape the square even.

12. Scribe or mark the other end. This square will be 11 × 11 mm and allow for the opposing latch to be inserted.

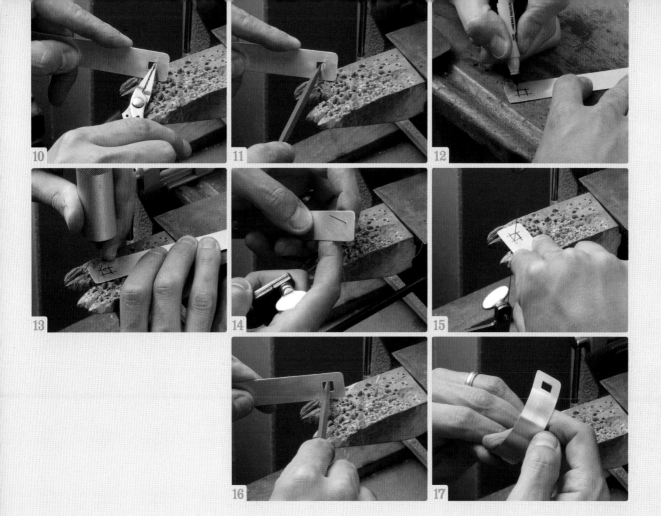

13. Again, drill out pilot holes at the corners. You can drill out as few as one corner or all four.

14. Pass the saw blade again back through the piece. This technique is called piercing.

15. Using the saw, cut the hole completely out. Do not leave a tab on this end.

16. Again, use needle files to clean up the inside of the hole. Use flat needle files to create crisp corners and a symmetrical square.

17. Shape the bracelet by hand or use a rawhide mallet to shape it on a bracelet mandrel. For this project, texture was added to the surface using the back side of a chasing hammer on a staking tool.

Wisdom
PROJECT: **Earrings**

These earrings are a showcase for unconventional materials; in this case, wisdom teeth. Any keepsakes, sentimental or novel items, and small objects can be incorporated into this jewelry design. Here you learn to create enclosures for and secure reclaimed or recycled material, refining your soldering, sawing, and filing skills to create personal (and curious!) jewelry.

TOOLS

- Scribe
- Jeweler's saw
- Files
- Flat-osed pliers
- Jeweler's snips
- Flux
- Soldering tweezers
- Soldering torch set
- Firebrick
- Soldering pick
- Copper tongs
- Pickle solution
- Sanding sticks (medium and fine)
- Flexible-shaft tool
- Drill bit set
- Side cutters
- Scouring pad

MATERIALS

- 24- and 26-gauge sterling silver sheet metal
- 18- and 20-gauge sterling silver wire
- Sterling silver sheet solder (medium and hard)
- Wisdom teeth or other organic material such as bone or antler
- Black patina solution

INSTRUCTIONS

Shaping

1. Using a ½ inch (1.3 cm) strip of 24-gauge sterling sheet, score a 45-degree angle with your scribe on opposing sides of your section.

2. Using your jeweler's saw, cut the sections at your marks. Be sure to hold to your lines; wavy and misaligned cuts are difficult to solder.

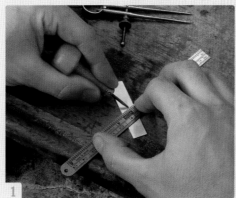

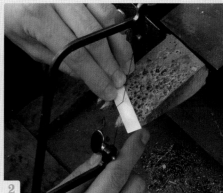

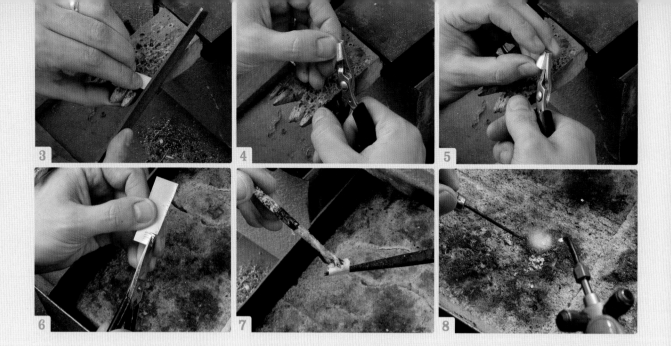

3. File the edges of your sheet metal flush. The ends should be square and able to create a seamless joint.

4. Using your flat-nosed pliers, begin to bend your piece into a cone shape, bringing both ends to a flush joint.

5. Complete the cone shape with your flat-nosed pliers. Keep the flush edges as close as possible creating a tight seam.

Soldering

6. Prepare to solder the joint by cutting three or four chips of hard solder. Paint your chips with flux.

7. Place your cone shape in the soldering tweezers joint side up. Paint with flux.

8. Begin by warming your chips of fluxed solder. Once heated they will ball up and be suspended in a pool of flux. Do not continue to heat; the honey-like effect of the warm flux enables you to pick them up with your soldering pick and place them on your joint.

9. Pick the balls up one by one and place them along your joint. If your flux has cooled and hardened, reheat with your torch. Do not heat to the point that your solder flows again.

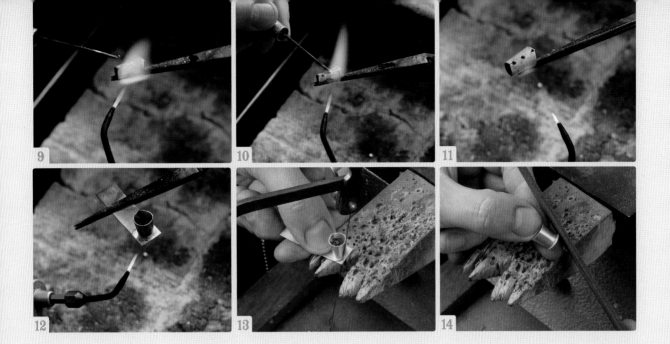

10. Continue placing solder along your joint. Three small pieces should work.

11. Once all of your solder is in place, heat the entire piece until the solder flows again, then quickly remove the flame. Overheating at this step will melt your work. Your piece should now be soldered. Remove from soldering tweezers with copper tongs and place in the pickle pot for about five minutes. Rinse and dry.

12. After filing the top of your cone flat, place on a strip of 24-gauge sterling sheet. Repeat the soldering process this time using medium solder chips. Solder this joint, then pickle, rinse, and dry.

Finishing

13. Using your jeweler's saw, cut out the cup shape, leaving a little lip around the perimeter.

14. File away your saw marks around the outside of the piece. File away the triangular shape from the lip of your cup. File and sand all areas to clean up your piece.

15. Test-fit the tooth and mark your hole. Then, using a 2.0 mm bit, drill out the holes on both sides.

16. Reinsert your tooth and using your drill, mark your holes on the tooth.

17. Remove the tooth from the piece and drill out. Remember to use a very slow speed. Drilling too fast in this organic material will create heat that causes a foul smell. Make sure your hole is level.

18. Using flattened 18-gauge wire, solder on a bail. For this project a tiny square shape was used.

19. Make the holding pins by balling up the ends of a piece of 18-gauge wire.

20. After cooling, cut the wire in half to create even headpins.

21. Test-fit all your parts again. You can make corrections by re-drilling your holes if necessary.

22. Trim your holding pin or headpin at about ¼ inch (6 mm) using side cutters.

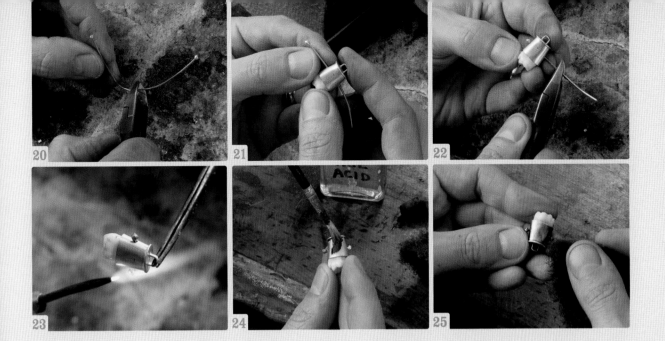

23. Place your work back in the soldering tweezers to ball up the other side. Now, using a harsh, fuel-starved and hissing flame, heat only the tip of the wire. Keep the flame away from the rest of the piece. Work quickly and remove the flame once the ball has been made.

24. Begin to paint the piece with black patina solution. Be careful not to get solution on your skin. Completely paint all of the surface area.

25. Complete the piece by using a scouring pad. Scuff away the surface treatment to reveal a matte finish. Continue to desired brightness.

26. Repeat steps 1 through 25 for the second earring, then create ear hooks from 20-gauge wire. Do not paint patina solution on the ear wires because it can irritate your skin.

| TIP | **Design Variations** |

Try making longer or shorter cones to accommodate other materials. Use other metals such as copper, brass, or gold. Teardrop-shaped glass or stone beads with horizontal drilled holes, wood, rubber, or plastic will also work. The design offers infinite variations if you alter the earrings and the objects enclosed within the cone.

Wire-Worked
PROJECT: # Earrings

These earrings use wire and simple forging to create unique, three-dimensional forms. Simple wire can be worked a variety of ways and this project uses them all: forging with a hammer, melting with a torch, forming with pliers, and finishing with a solder joint.

TOOLS

- Side cutters
- Third hand
- Soldering tweezers
- Soldering torch set
- Firebrick
- Chasing hammer
- Steel bench block or anvil
- Flexible-shaft tool
- Drill bit set
- Scribe or punch
- Flat-nosed pliers
- Round-nosed pliers
- Flux
- Soldering pick
- Copper tongs
- Pickle solution
- Sanding sticks
- Scouring pad

MATERIALS

- 24" (61 cm) length of 18-gauge sterling silver wire
- 12" (30.5 cm) length of 20-gauge sterling silver wire
- Sterling silver sheet solder (medium or easy)
- Patina solution

INSTRUCTIONS

Shaping

1. Using side cutters, cut your 18-gauge wire into 3-inch (7.6 cm) pieces. For this project, each earring has three sections of this wire, so you need a total of six sections. It is a good idea to cut one extra just in case.

2. Secure the sections in the third hand. Securing the sections as shown minimizes movement and the potential for two sections fusing together. Using a torch, heat the ends of the wire with a bushy blue flame until they begin to ball up. Be sure to do this over a firebrick in case a drop of molten metal falls. Gravity makes for nice round balls, so make sure the wire is pointed straight downward. Let cool or quench in water.

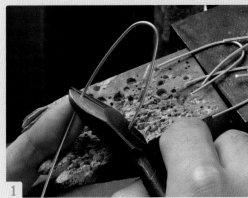

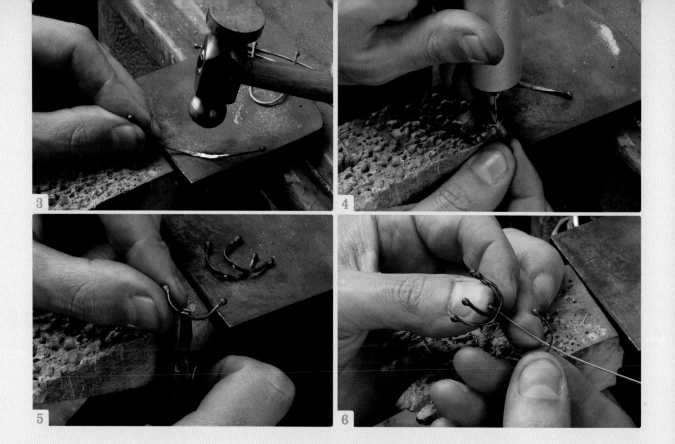

3. Open the sections straight and begin hammering them flat near the center. The ball end of a chasing hammer makes a nice surface texture. Be sure to hammer flat enough for a hole to be drilled. Taper your forging from the center to the ends.

4. Once the sections have been forged flat, drill a hole in each one. Because the earring wire portion will be made of 20-gauge wire, a size 65 bit is used. Measure and mark your hole using a scribe or punch.

5. Begin shaping your parts using round- or flat-nosed pliers. U shapes are formed carefully, because the metal is weakened in the center from drilling.

6. Slide your sections onto a headpin made of 20-gauge wire. Usually, if a shorter section is present, it is installed first. Install longer sections last.

Soldering

7. Once the work is set and evenly spaced, place the work in the third hand. Solder with medium or easy solder. Be sure to solder all the pieces together as well as the headpin. These are rigid earrings with no kinetic movement. If you wish to have yours swing and spin, solder all the parts, then slide onto the headpin. Using copper tongs, place the piece in pickle solution for about five minutes, then rinse with water.

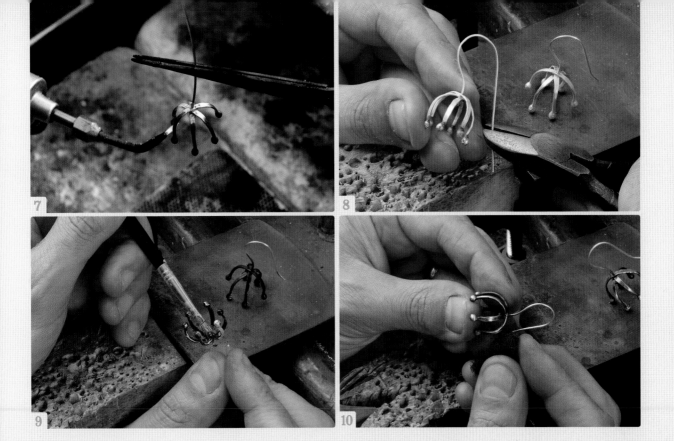

Finishing

8. Create the shape of the earwire using round-nosed pliers, then measure and trim with side cutters. Be sure to sand and polish the end of the earwire smooth so it does not irritate the wearer's ear.

9. Paint the piece with patina solution. Carefully, cover the entire piece except for the earwire. Residue from patina can sometime irritate the wearer's ear holes. Always rinse the piece in cool water to remove any chemical residue and wash hands with soap and water.

10. Finish the piece to desired brightness using a scouring pad. The patina solution will be removed with more scrubbing action leaving a bright silver, matte finish.

> ### TIP | Make It Your Own
>
> Try altering this design to meet your personal taste. You can try adding a hinge to create kinetic movement, or elongate the sections of wire to make a more dramatic shape. You can also forgo the soldering step, and add a few spacer beads to the headpin to change up the design.

Gallery

Original, artistic, and inventive jewelry gets noticed. When designs are created that have smart mechanics, innovative techniques, and integrate smooth functions, stunning jewelry is created. The gallery showcases the work of some of the world's best jewelry designers. These well-respected professionals set the bar for the trends both in the art and fashion community.

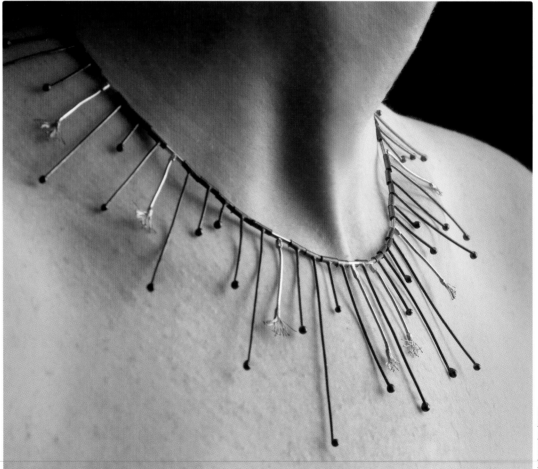

Artist: Andrea Williams
Title: *Kebyar Autumn Necklace*
Materials: sterling silver, 18-karat gold
Techniques: Unknown

LEFT
Artist: Colleen Baran
Title: *I Miss You* from the *Like Wearing a Love Letter* series
Materials: Sterling silver, rubber
Techniques: Soldered, set

BELOW LEFT
Artist: Courtney Anne Poole
Title: *Spaghetti Brooch*
Materials: Fine silver filigree
Techniques: Silver filigree

BELOW RIGHT
Artist: Brandon Holschuh
Title: *Bird Ring*
Materials: Sterling, opaque agate, paper
Techniques: Soldered, bezel set, distressed

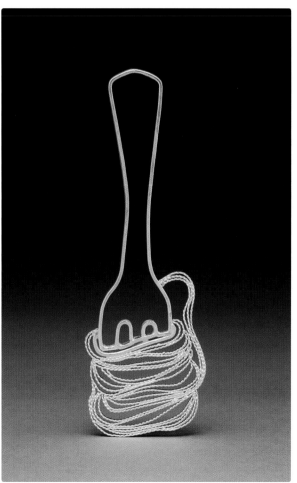

TOP LEFT
Artist: Justin Klocke
Title: *Cufflinks*
Materials: sterling silver
Techniques: fabricated, die formed

TOP RIGHT
Artists: Roberta and David Williamson
Title: *Boy Scout*
Materials: sterling silver, antique pin-back button, vintage pocket knife, compass
Techniques: fabricated, cast, bezel set, soldered, patinaed

BELOW
Artist: Courtney Anne Poole
Title: *Medicine Locket*
Materials: nickel silver, aluminum, rubber
Techniques: Dapped circles, soldered

Photo: George Ensley

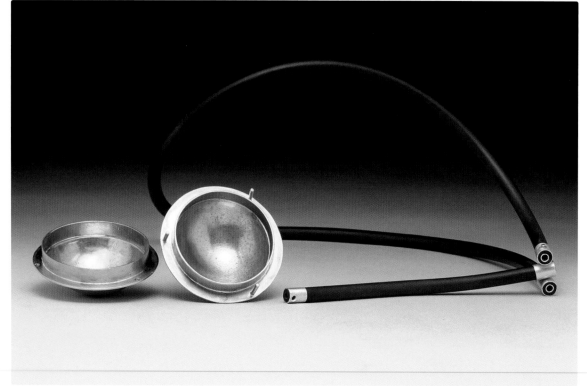

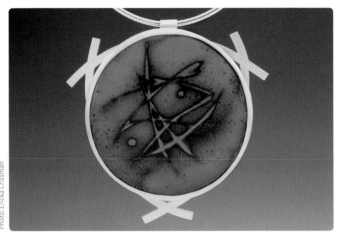

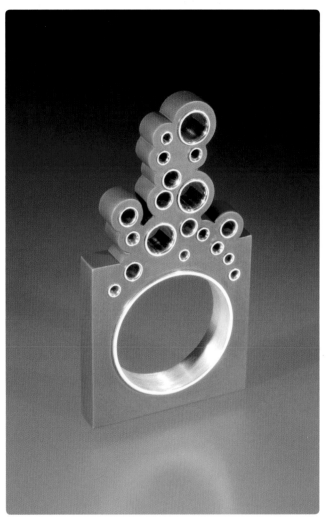

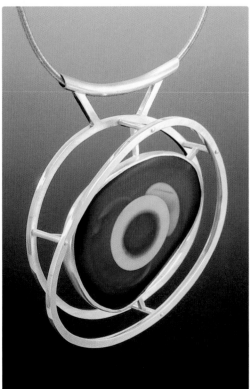

TOP LEFT
Artist: L Sue Szabo
Title: *Sticks and Stones*
Materials: sterling silver, copper, enamel
Techniques: fabricated, bezel set, riveted, enamel stoned matte

TOP RIGHT
Artist: Jon Ryan
Title: *Bubble Ring*
Materials: aluminum, sterling silver
Techniques: carved, anodized, fabricated

BOTTOM
Artist: Linda Sue Szabo
Title: *Splash*
Materials: sterling silver, imperial jasper
Techniques: forged, bezel set, riveted, hand fabricated

TOP
Artist: Wes Airgood
Title: *Rings For the Upset and Adrift*
Materials: copper, sterling silver
Techniques: Unknown

BOTTOM
Artist: Susan Skoczen
Title: *Knoll's Edge*
Materials: Sterling, paint
Techniques: Soldered, fabricated

TOP
Artist: Peg Fetter
Title: *Forged Bangle Bracelets*
Materials: Steel, 14-karat gold
Techniques: Forged, oxidized, heat rivets

BOTTOM LEFT
Artist: Peg Fetter
Title: *Cross Ring*
Materials: Steel, 14-karat gold
Techniques: Heat oxidized, gold inlay, fabricated, soldered

BOTTOM RIGHT
Artist: Brandon Holschuh
Title: *Ditrichum Pallidum in Fruiting*
Materials: electroformed copper, sterling silver, live moss
Techniques: riveted, soldered, forged, electroformed copper, fabricated

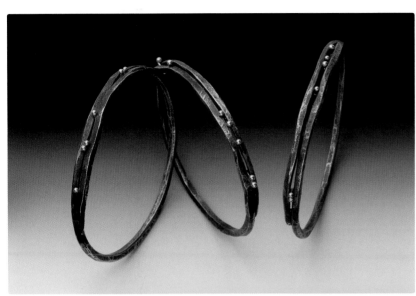

Photo: Don Casper

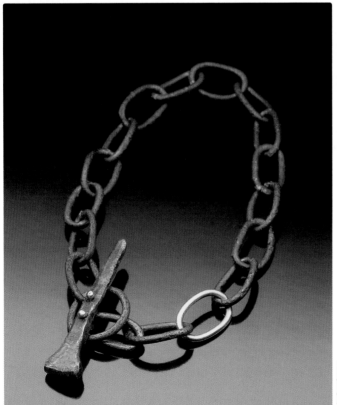

Photo: Don Casper

Courtesy of K. Van Meter

TOP
Artist: Debra Rosen
Title: *Prehinite Ring*
Materials: Sterling, prehinite
Techniques: Fabricated, constructed,
soldered, fused

BOTTOM
Artist: Andrea Williams
Title: *Kebyar Triple Earrings*
Materials: Sterling
Techniques: Fused, soldered, fabricated,
domed

Photo: Dan Fox

Photo: markcraig.com

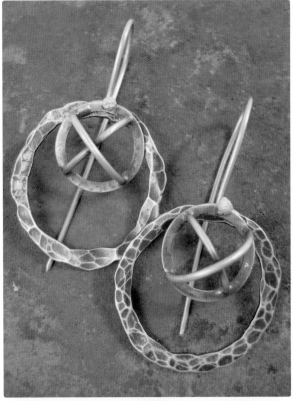

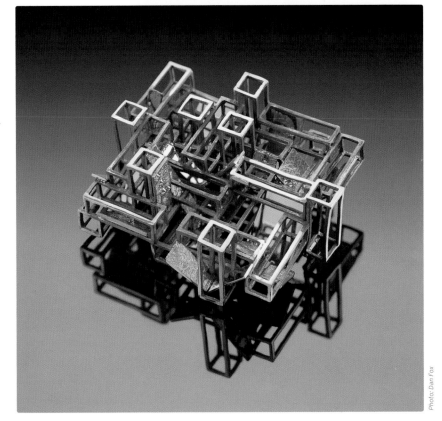

Photo: Dan Fox

TOP LEFT
Artist: Brandon Holschuh
Title: *Earrings*
Materials: Sterling, brass
Techniques: Soldered, forged, fabricated, oxidized

TOP RIGHT
Artist: Brandon Holschuh
Title: *Untitled*
Materials: Serpentine, sterling
Techniques: Riveted, cold connected, soldered, fabricated, constructed

BOTTOM
Artist: Todd Pownell
Title: *Architectural Nest*
Materials: Diamonds, gold, sterling
Techniques: Fabricated, constructed, soldered, fused

Photo: markcraig.com

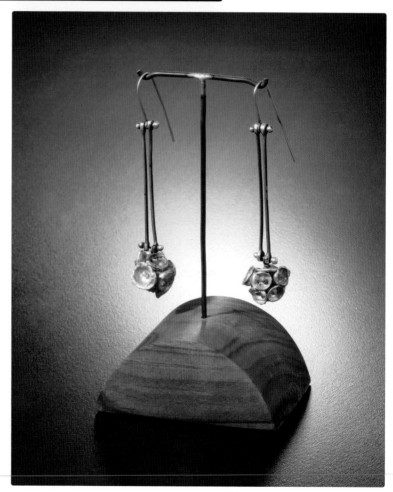

TOP
Artist: Andrea Williams
Title: *Kebyar Bimetal Pendant*
Materials: sterling silver, 22-karat gold bi-metal
Techniques: Fused, soldered, domed

BOTTOM
Artist: Brandon Holschuh
Title: *Gravity Earrings*
Materials: Sterling
Techniques: Gravity formed, forged, torch worked

Photo: Doug Yaple

LEFT
Artist: Sarah Hood
Title: *Malden Avenue East*
Materials: Sterling, Chinese lantern pods
Techniques: Soldered, fabricated

BELOW LEFT
Artist: Brandon Holschuh
Title: *Untitled*
Materials: Sterling, chalcedony
Techniques: Chased, forged

BELOW RIGHT
Artist: Brandon Holschuh
Title: *Recycled Pendant*
Materials: Reclaimed glass, recycled sterling
Techniques: Forged, chased, soldered

Photo: Michelle Bonnay

Photo: Michelle Bonnay

APPENDIX: Beyond the Studio

Most jewelry designs begin with a concept—a mechanism, a color, a material, anything that sparks a whim. Translating that concept into a physical piece of jewelry (or art) is the essence of the designing process. No matter how well-stocked your studio is, your mind is still your strongest, most reliable tool.

The more original work you generate, the more you will develop an individual design language. As you hone specialized techniques, processes, or materials, your trademark style will emerge.

Artist: Dan Cook
Title: *Milky Way Identification Device*
Materials: Brass, silver, plastic, light emitting diodes, touch circuit, nocturnal solar engine
Techniques: Constructed, cast, fabricated, soldered

Pursuing Your Career in Jewelry

Once you have refined your designs and are communicating with a unique design language, you can start to consider pursuing a career in jewelry. There are many different avenues—and degrees of commitment—to explore.

EDUCATIONAL OPPORTUNITIES

Specialized technical schools Vocational-style programs improve your skill set and refine your techniques in anything from jewelry repair to advanced stone setting. For the devoted and ambitious, many institutions offer a range of degrees in their metalsmithing programs.

Studio workshops and art centers Many communities have jeweler's workshops, studios, and art centers that offer short-term classes Colleges offer a regular arts workshop schedule—especially intensive sessions during the summer—and many of the most popular sessions are on jewelry.

Join an organization More often than not, there are organizations in or near your hometown. Organizations and groups are a great support system for sharing and gathering information. Most require a minimal membership fee, but the benefits far outweigh the costs. Many provide special services and discounts for goods and services for members only.

EARNING A LIVING IN THE JEWELRY BUSINESS

Bench jewelers Fine jewelry stores are always looking for bench jewelers to work behind the scenes to hand-craft pieces of others' design. Working as a bench jeweler, you will be immersed in the manufacturing side of the craft, which can be a pro or a con. If you have developed your own design language, you might chafe against reproducing the works of others. If you haven't, reproducing the work of others will improve your skill set and build your confidence.

Working for yourself Remaining gainfully self-employed as a jeweler opens a whole different side of the craft business. Full time, part time, or "freelance," you can be as immersed in it as you want. For art jewelers, going into business for yourself will take you to retail shows, art markets, and galleries. Your sales venues could include internet sales, websites, and custom orders, all of which come when you decide to go into business for yourself.

 Business Tips for Self-Employed Artists

- Always sell your work as a desirable product and market yourself as a professional artist.

- Take a class in small business administration to acquire or brush up on your business acumen. Visit your local small business association for advice and direction.

- Keep watertight records of inventory and costs incurred, both for material and supplies. Be sure your accounting and sales records are flawless.

- Talk to and network with other professionals… constantly; know what you are getting yourself into.

Resources

Books

Codina, Carles.
*The Complete Book
of Jewelry Making*
Asheville (NC): Lark Books, 1999
ISBN 1-57990-188-3

Foote, Theodore P.
*Jewelry Making:
A Guide for Beginners*
Worcester (MA): Davis
Publications, 1981
ISBN 0-87192-130-8

Gollberg, Joanna. *The Art
and Craft of Jewelry Making*
Asheville (NC): Lark Books, 2006
ISBN 1-57990-570-6

Gollberg, Joanna.
Making Metal Jewelry
Asheville (NC): Lark Books, 2003
ISBN 1-57990-347-9

McCreight, Tim.
*The Complete Metalsmith:
An Illustrated Handbook*
New York (NY): Sterling
Publishing, 1991
ISBN 0-87192-240-1

McGrath, Jinks.
*The Encyclopedia of Jewelry
Making Techniques*
Philadelphia/London: Running
Press, 1995
ISBN 1-56138-526-3

Neumann, Robert Von.
*The Design and
Creation of Jewelry*
Philadelphia and New York:
Chilton Books, 1961

Olver, Elizabeth.
Jewelry Making Techniques Book
Cincinnati (OH): North Light
Books, 2001
ISBN 1-58180-210-2

Stokes, Gordon.
Jewelry Making
New York: Drake Publishers, 1973
ISBN 0-87749-562-9

Untracht, Oppi.
*Jewelry Concepts
and Technology*
New York: Doubleday
and Company, 1982
ISBN 0-385-04185-3

Online Resources
for Jewelry Making

**The American Craft
Council (ACC)**
www.craftcouncil.org

**The Association for
Contemporary Jewelry (ACJ)**
www.acj.org.uk

Ganoskin
www.ganoksin.com

Klimt02
www.klimt02.net

Society of Arts and Crafts
www.societyofcrafts.org

**The Society of North American
Goldsmiths (SNAG)**
www.snagmetalsmith.org

Art Jewelry Galleries

Aaron Faber Gallery
New York, NY, United States
www.aaronfaber.com

Antherea
Barcelona, Spain
www.antherea.com

Bellagio
Asheville, NC, United States
www.bellagioarttowear.com

Charon Kransen Arts
New York, NY, United States
www.charonkransenarts.com

Facere Jewelry Art
Seattle, WA, United States
www.facerejewelryart.com

Freehand Gallery
Los Angeles, CA, United States
www.freehand.com

Galerie Caroline Van Hoek
Brussels, Belgium
www.carolinevanhoek.be

Galerie ra
Amsterdam, Netherlands
www.galerie-ra.nl

Galerie Rob Koudijs
Amsterdam, Netherlands
www.galerierobkoudijs.nl

Gallery Deux Poissons
Tokyo, Japan
www.deuxpoissons.com

Gallery Flux
San Francisco, CA, United States
www.galleryflux.com

Gallery Loupe
Montclair, NJ, United States
www.galleryloupe.com

Gallery M
Cleveland, OH, United States
www.gallerymjewelry.com

Jewelers Werk
Washington, DC, United States
www.jewelerswerk.com

Lesley Craze Gallery
London, United Kingdom
www.lesleycrazegallery.co.uk

Lingg Showroom
Woodmere, OH, United States
www.lingg.us

Mobilia Gallery
Cambridge, MA, United States
www.mobilia-gallery.com

Obsidian Gallery
Tucson, AZ, United States
www.obsidian-gallery.com

Ornamentum Gallery
Hudson, NY, United States
www.ornamentumgallery.com

Patina Gallery
Santa Fe, NM, United States
www.patina-gallery.com

Sienna Gallery
Lenox, MA, United States
www.siennagallery.com

Shibumi Gallery
Berkeley, CA, United States
www.shibumigallery.com

Silke & The Gallery
Antwerp, Belgium
www.silkefleischer.com

**Society of Arts And
Crafts Gallery**
Boston, MA, United States
www.societyofcrafts.org

Thomas Mann Gallery I/O
New Orleans, LA, United States
www.thomasmann.com

Velvet da Vinci
San Francisco, CA, United States
www.velvetdavinci.com

Jewelry Publications

American Craft Magazine
Published six times per year
by the American Craft Council
www.americancraftmag.org

American Style Magazine
Baltimore, MD, United States
Published monthly
www.americanstyle.com

Art Jewelry Magazine
Published bimonthly
Waukesha, WI, United States
www.artjewelrymag.com

Lapidary Journal Jewelry Artist
Published monthly
Loveland, CO, United States
www.lapidaryjournal.com

Metalsmith Magazine
Publication of the Society of North
American Goldsmiths (SNAG);
published five times per year
Eugene, OR, United States
www.snagmetalsmith.org

Ornament Magazine
Published five times per year
San Marcos, CA, United States
www.ornamentmagazine.com

Suppliers

Fire Mountain Gems
Grants Pass, OR, United States
www.firemountaingems.com
Supplier of faceted gemstones,
beads, mountings, settings, and
accessories

Otto Frei
Oakland, CA, United States
www.ottofrei.com
Extensive selection of jewelers'
tools, supplies, and equipment

Rio Grande
Albuquerque, NM, United States
www.riogrande.com
Supplier of tools, raw materials,
gemstones, and more—wholesale
and retail

Sierra Pacific Casting
Oakland, CA, United States
www.sierrapacificcasting.com
Precious metals casting services

Stuller
Lafayette, LA, United States
www.stuller.com
Manufacturer and supplier of
finished jewelry, raw materials,
tools, supplies, equipment and
books on jewelry; excellent source
for wire, sheet, solder, and general
equipment and tools

Glossary

Alloys Combinations or mixtures of nonferrous metals

Annealing The process of heating metal to a cherry-red color and maintaining the temperature to reposition the molecular structure of the metal's composition. Annealing softens metal, which prepares it for shaping, forming, and other techniques.

Arkansas stone A small, rectangular-prism-shaped stone used to shape and sharpen gravers or knives; typically used with mineral oil.

Bead-setting tool set A set of pointed steel tools, each with a different-shaped depression, used to create a head of metal called a bead. The bead head mimics a prong when used to set gemstones.

Bench pin A wooden wedge-shaped block that is attached to a jeweler's bench designed to support objects for working with hand tools.

Bezel A type of setting that uses a single continuous band of metal to secure the object or stone.

Bezel pusher A polished steel tool used to fold and crimp a bezel around the perimeter of a stone; usually set in a wooden handle

Binding wire Iron wire used to bind objects to prepare for soldering. Wire is made of iron and has a higher melting point than precious metals, so it can tolerate excessive heat from soldering without fusing to the metals to be joined.

Buffer/polishing cabinet Studio equipment that keeps airborne particles contained and out of circulation with a filtration system (a vent hood and air filter)

Buffs Muslin, felt, or leather wheels used in conjunction with a buffing motor or lathe. Polishing compounds are applied directly to the face of the wheel during the polishing process.

Burnisher A highly polished steel tool used to smooth and polish metal around the perimeter of bezel-set stones

Casting The process of creating a metal object from a wax model

Chasing The process of texturing or indenting the surface of metal with variously shaped tools and a hammer

Chasing hammer A jeweler's hammer used for striking a punch, stamp, or chasing tool that makes an indention or impression on a metal surface

Cold Connection The process of joining metal without the use of solders or heat, such as with rivets, tabs, or screws

Cutters Any tool designed to cut metal, wire, or other material; primarily a hand tool

Dapping punches Polished steel tools used with a doming block to create rounded dome shapes

Disc-cutting tool A tool set designed to repeatedly cut precise circles of various sizes.

Doming block A square steel, brass, or wooden block with dome-shaped depressions used with dapping punches to create rounded dome shapes

Drawing The process of elongating a wire's length, narrowing its diameter, or changing its shape by pulling it through a series of holes in a drawplate.

Drawplate A metal plate with various-sized and various-shaped holes through which wire can be drawn

Enamel A powderlike substance fired in a kiln that binds to the surface of metal. Once fired, it becomes a glasslike coating; available in many colors.

Escapement file A specialty file used to avoid scratching of surfaces around the work area of the file face. Escapement files have a smooth side (on the reverse) to prevent file marks on adjoining surfaces

Firebrick A fire-resistant material used as a heat barrier inside of kilns and used by jewelers as a soldering surface

Firescale A blueish haze on the surface of metal created during torch firing; most commonly, it is due to an oxidation of copper content in sterling silver.

Flexible shaft A rotary-style tool with a flexible shaft attached to a motor controlled by a variable speed foot pedal. The flexible shaft tool can be fitted with various attachments to drill, grind, and polish

Flux A substance used in the soldering (or welding) process to clean the surfaces to be joined; also aids in the flow of solder at the joint

Forging The act of using a tool (most often a hammer) to stretch, manipulate, and distort the metal from its original shape, such as flattening wire

Forming The act of changing a metal's shape without displacing its mass or surface area, such as simple bending.

Gravers Various-shaped steel tools used to engrave the surface of metal or to set stones.

Investment A plasterlike substance used to encapsulate a wax model in a flask in preparation for casting

Kiln Equipment used to heat contents at specific temperatures for extended periods of time. Kilns are used in the jeweler's studio for casting, enameling, and the firing of precious metal clays

Needle files Miniature files in assorted shapes used for intricate detail work in metal and other materials; available in square, barette, crossed, half-round, knife, triangle, and three-square shapes

Nippers A hand tool designed for flush cuts against flat surfaces

Non-ferrous metal Metals that do not contain iron

Patina A fine coating of oxides, usually copper sulfate on the surface of metal; synonymous with the blue-green color found on old bronze objects

Pickle A chemical solution made of sodium bisulfate that aids in the removal of surface oxides and flux residue due to soldering

Rawhide mallet A mallet made of rawhide designed to be firm enough to shape metal with blunt force, but soft enough to not leave a surface impression

Ring clamp A wooden or plastic hand tool designed to function with a wedge inserted in the end to create a hold on an object, typically a ring. The jaws may be lined with leather to prevent marring of the surface of the work.

Rolling mill A steel bench-top tool that uses pressure to flatten or roll sheet metal

Rouge A polishing compound used for a final polish of metal during finishing

Shear A bench-top cutting tool designed to make flush, straight-line cuts in sheet metal.

Silversmith hammer A specialty hammer designed to work sheet metal into shapes; available in styles including raising, creasing, planishing, and embossing

Solder An alloy of metals designed to melt and flow at temperatures lower than precious metals, which allows for creating secure metal bonds

Soldering To join, link, or connect metal with a joint and the use of solder and heat

Sprue A stemlike shape that is the base of a wax model or the opening in a rubber or silicone mold in which molten metal enters the cavity

Sweeps catch A removable tray-style drawer attached to a jeweler's workbench designed to catch filings, cuttings, and other material; usually lined or stretched with fabric or leather

Third hand Counterlocking tweezers affixed to a heavy base used to hold or suspend work during soldering

Tripoli A polishing compound for fast cutting of metal during finishing

Tube-cutting jig A tool designed for cutting tubing and wire to specific lengths

Vulcanizer A heated bench-top press used to form rubber molds during duplication casting techniques

Watchmaker's bench A workbench frequently used by jewelers as an alternative to a standard jeweler's style bench. This style bench has more storage drawers and does not have a cut-out work top.

Index

Artist Directory

Wesley C. Airgood
Athens, GA 30605
www.airgoodmetals.com

Colleen Baran
Surrey BC V4N 2V3 Canada
www.ColleenBaran.com

Grace Chin
Shaker Heights, OH 44122 USA
www.gracechindesign.com

Daniel Cook
New Bedford, MA 02743 USA
damndan@gmail.com

Peg Fetter
St. Louis, MO 63110 USA
www.pegfetter.com

Brandon Holschuh
Concord Township, OH 44060
www.brandonholschuh.com

Sarah Hood
Seattle, WA 98103 USA
www.sarahhoodjewelry.com

Justin Klocke
Minturn, CO 81645 USA
www.justinklocke.com

Victoria Lansford
Atlanta, GA 30312 USA
www.victorialansford.com

Timothy Lazure
Greenville, NC 27858 USA
lazuret@ecu.edu

Courtney Anne Poole
Athens, GA 30606
cap _ art@windstream.net

Todd A. Pownell
Cleveland, OH 4103
www.tapstudios.com

Debra A. Rosen
Cleveland, OH 44103 USA
www.tapstudios.com

Jon Ryan
Wheaton, IL 60187 USA
www.jonryan.com

Susan Skoczen
Fairport Harbor, OH 44077 USA
www.susanskoczen.com

L. Sue Szabo
Toledo, OH 43623 USA
sueszabo@bex.net

Andrea Williams
Weymouth, MA 02189 USA
www.boundearth.com

Roberta and David Williamson
Berea, OH 44017 USA
pawgu@aol.com

Acknowledgments

First and foremost I want to thank my beautiful wife, Michelle, and my dearest daughter, Meena, who have supported and encouraged my journey to becoming a full-time studio jeweler and now an author. I could have never accomplished any of these things without the complete support of my family. Your help and patience with me is treasured. This is to all the late nights, lost weekends, and missed moments. I love you both. (To quote Kristin Müller; "It's not easy to have a dad inspired to the point of distraction.")

I also would like to thank my parents, Rita and Robert. They never stopped believing that I could succeed as an artist. I am forever grateful for the encouragement and support over the years. No matter what my endeavors have been, they have always helped me succeed. I am proud to have such wonderful, loving parents.

Thank you to my high school art teacher, Ms. Phyllis Fannin, who opened my eyes to the world of art and jewelry. Her direction and encouragement have had an impact on my life and my work that can't be put into words.

Special thanks to Dan Cook, who has always challenged me to be my best. I have the pleasure of calling him a true friend. Thanks for all the good times—there are more to come.

To Derre Buike for tolerating me and enabling my livelihood by teaching me to be business minded.

To Todd Pownell and Debra Rosen for their bench tricks and helping me to refine my skills. You are an inspiration, and you have a great thing going.

Thanks to Mary Ann Hall, for striking up the conversation with me that led to this book. Thanks also to Jeff Yost, Heidi Lingg, Mark Yasenchak, Jamie Drysdale, and Terry and Karen Miller for inspiring me to take chances.

Special thanks to Rochelle Bourgault, my editor, for allowing me such freedom to make this project so great and to Dan Morgan, for countless hours in the studio and for more countless hours behind the wheel. Your trained eye helped me communicate my vision through photos.

Finally, thanks to all my family and friends, to everyone who supports me through my jewelry, and to Nance Hikes, for allowing me to share her teeth with the world.

About
the Author

Brandon Holschuh has been a jeweler for nearly 20 years and maintains an active jeweler's studio in Concord Township, Ohio. He is a member of the Society of North American Goldsmiths, The American Craft Council, and the Society of Arts and Crafts. An accomplished exhibitor, winning numerous awards and merits, he maintains a demanding, year-round show schedule. In between shows, he teaches the fundamentals of jewelry fabrication to students in small class groups in his studio and holds workshops at nearby art centers. Visit www.brandonholschuh.com for more information.